ASTON MARTIN

The Legend

ASTON MARTIN
The Legend

Michael Bowler

p

Page 1: This special badge was created for the second generation Zagato Astons; it was first seen on the Vantage Zagato at its 1986 launch. Page 2: The first generation Zagato Aston was launched in 1960; this car has the first chassis number of the 19 cars built at the time. Page 3: From the second series of 1.5-litre models, this is a 1933 Le Mans 2/4-seater which took part in the 1934 Mille Miglia – just room for two small adults on a short run.

This is a Parragon book
This edition published in 2004

Copyright © Parragon 1997

Parragon
Queen Street House
4 Queen Street
Bath BA1 1HE, UK

Designed, produced and packaged by
Stonecastle Graphics Ltd

Edited by Philip de Ste. Croix

ISBN 1-40544-332-4

Printed in Indonesia

Figures and data in this book are quoted in the originally recorded measurements first, with the metric/imperial equivalents noted in brackets.

Photographic credits:

All photographs by **Neill Bruce Motoring Photolibrary**, with the exception of the following: *(Abbreviations: r = right, l = left, t = top, b = below)*

Aston Martin Lagonda Ltd. & The Peter Roberts Collection/Neill Bruce: 6(*l*), 6 (*r*), 59, 61(*b*).

David Hawtin: 8, 9(*l*), 9(*r*).

David Hodges: 78

Roger Stowers: 45(*t*), 45(*b*), 52, 53(*t*), 53(*b*), 79(*t*).

The Aston Martin Owner's Club Archives: 7.

Michael Bowler: 79(*b*).

Neill Bruce and the publishers would like to thank all of the owners who have made their cars available for photography, especially the following:

Mike Barker at The Midland Motor Museum: DB Mk III saloon, blue DB5, 1978 V8 Vantage, Prince of Wales spec V8 Volante and Vantage Zagato.

Brooks Auctioneers: DBR2/1.

DB7 Volante photographed at **David Barnett's Purston Manor Farm.**

Nigel Dawes: 1933 Le Mans, 'The Black Car' 2-litre, 2-litre sports (DB1), early DB2 in race trim, DB2/4 saloon and convertible, Project 215 and DB4 convertible.

Dr. Dudley Heath: International, Mk II saloon and Ulster.

Philip Jones of Byron Garages Ltd: blue DB2, blue DB4 GT Zagato, blue DB6 Mk 2.

The Earl of March for the wonderful Goodwood Festival of Speed.

Dr. Tom Rollason: 15/98 saloon, 'The Atom' prototype photographed courtesy of Birmingham Botanical Gardens & Glasshouses.

Special thanks to Aston Martin Lagonda's historian **Roger Stowers**; good friend, photographer and patient 'positioner' of each hand-crafted creation.

Contents

Introduction

THAT Aston Martin should still be making cars, 80 years after the first one was registered, is a remarkable tribute to all the enthusiasts who have kept it going beyond the call of historical duty or financial sense; starry-eyed new owners, dedicated engineer-designers, and the faithful craftsmen have all played their part in continuing to produce the charismatic cars that have appealed to generations of sporting motorists.

Above: Aston Martin co-founder Robert Bamford.

Until the 1987 arrival of the Ford Motor Company, Aston Martin had mostly been owned by people and companies with little previous experience of the motor industry. Even David Brown was only familiar with tractors before he guided the company through its longest one-owner period. And none of them could ever be said to have emerged financially richer for the experience.

First away was Lionel Martin, who, with Robert Bamford had competed with a Singer in speed hill-climbs just before the First World War. Although Bamford had served an engineering apprenticeship, Martin was just a sporting motorist whose family was involved in mining; but, together they ran a garage business in London's Chelsea, a general repair garage with an agency for Singers. Rather than continue to compete with modified Singers, Martin decided that they should build their own car. It was Martin's name that was coupled to the name of one of those hill-climbs – Aston Hill – to produce Aston Martin.

Many parts were being made for the new car during 1914 but the engine was available before the rest of the car was completed. Basically a modified 1389cc Coventry Simplex engine with side valves, this was installed in a 1908 Isotta Fraschini to serve as a mobile test bed. However, the rest of the parts eventually arrived and the car was completed in early 1915, running a considerable mileage over the next four years as the first prototype. It was known as the Coal Scuttle, apparently due to its body shape,

Above: Co-founder Lionel Martin was the one who put Aston Martin into production. Right: Martin had been gone 10 years when this shot was taken in 1935 at Feltham where Mark II models were being built.

but it was an attractive two-seater which was to become a familiar sight on the post-war competition scene.

However, the continuation of the First World War hampered any further progress on its successors until a year after hostilities had ceased. The second prototype was completed at the end of 1920 by which time Robert Bamford had lost interest in car production, and the Martins, husband and wife, took over and moved to fresh Kensington premises.

The production story starts here.

The Lionel Martin Series

WHILE the first car to be labelled as an Aston Martin had been registered for the road in 1915, it was the second car that was the true forerunner of the production cars that were to follow.

Like most cars of the period it had a simple twin-channel chassis with semi-elliptic leaf springs all round, and brakes were fitted to the rear wheels only. A four-speed gearbox was used. The 1389cc engine was fitted initially but by mid-1921 this had been redesigned by the former Coventry Simplex engine designer H.V. Robb, who had gone to work with the Martins. It was still a side-valve unit but the crankcase had three bearings instead of two, a gear-type oil pump replaced the previous plunger and the camshaft was driven by gears instead of by chain. Because Lionel Martin firmly believed that racing improved the breed, the engine capacity was increased to 1487cc by increasing the stroke with the new crankshaft. In this form the car achieved 72mph (116km/h) when *Motor* and *Autocar* tested it in 1921.

This should have been enough to justify the start of production but Martin's thoughts were still on competition. Robb designed a single ohc, 16-valve, 1.5-litre engine for this and it was raced in 1921 with Count Zborowski driving; he failed to beat a side-valve Aston Martin in the 1921 JCC 200-mile race. Zborowski brought in a twin-cam design from a Peugeot engineer but that fared little better in 1922. Although these racing specials failed to

Below: A classic vintage tourer with its long sweeping wings and a running board – this was built in 1924.

Below: The clover-leaf body style provided comfort for two with an extra seat below the boat deck hatch. Right: Large diameter front-wheel brakes are operated by Perrot shafts; the beam axle is controlled by semi-elliptic springing.

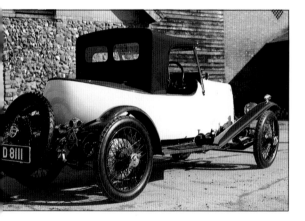

justify their expense, the side-valve engine was light and reliable; using one of these in a single seater, Aston Martin took a number of world records including 16 hours at 76mph (122km/h) in 1922.

Sanity began to prevail in 1923 when production effectively started, with the cars being built to the specification of that second prototype with the addition of front-wheel-brakes. At last the acquired expertise was to be used to earn the company some money to pay for the racing. Priced at £700-£750 according to the body design, they were very expensive for the time; as would be the continuing story for the next 70 years, quality came first, the price was a secondary consideration.

By 1924, though, Martin's resources were diminishing and he sold the assets to the Charnwood family, but it was too late and the company went into receivership for the first time in late 1925. Too much had been spent on racing and not enough on production preparation. The 50 cars sold over the period did not generate enough income to keep the company afloat.

They did, however, establish the Aston Martin name as synonymous with fine sporting automobiles as much at home on the road as in competition.

Production dates   1914-25

SPECIFICATION	1924 SPORTS
ENGINE	4-cylinder side-valve, 1486cc
HORSEPOWER	45bhp @ 4000rpm
TRANSMISSION	4-speed manual
CHASSIS	Steel channel, aluminium body
SUSPENSION	Beam/live axles on leaf springs
BRAKES	4-wheel drum brakes
TOP SPEED	72mph (116km/h)
ACCELERATION	0-50mph (80km/h): 25sec

Aston Martin International & Series One

THE COMPANY that came to the rescue was the Birmingham engine builders, Renwick and Bertelli. Italian-born Augustus Bertelli had been General Manager at Enfield-Allday Motors developing a new sporting car for which his brother Enrico built the coachwork. Production was under way and the company were competing against Aston Martin in the Brooklands 200-mile races when the firm went into liquidation due to the failure of the parent company in 1922.

Bertelli then had a spell working for Woolf Barnato on what might have been another sporting car, but that project too came to an end. He was then able to join up with W.S. Renwick; having considered car production, they decided to build engines for the motor industry. One of Renwick and Bertelli's first employees was Claude Hill who was to have considerable influence over Aston Martin engineering for many years. He designed a new single-overhead-camshaft, 1500cc, four-cylinder

engine; the big crankshaft had three main bearings and the camshaft was driven by chain from an intermediate gear. By 1926 this was being tested in an old Enfield-Allday chassis.

It was in 1926 that they were approached by the Charnwoods to advise on the future of Aston Martin. Bertelli still wanted to get into car production and reckoned that it was more cost effective to buy an established manufacturer than start from scratch. Although they discovered that

SPECIFICATION	1929 INTERNATIONAL
ENGINE	4-cylinder sohc, 1494cc
HORSEPOWER	56bhp @ 4250rpm
TRANSMISSION	4-speed manual
CHASSIS	Steel channel, aluminium body
SUSPENSION	Beam/live axles on leaf springs
BRAKES	4-wheel drum brakes
TOP SPEED	78mph (126km/h)
ACCELERATION	0-50mph (80km/h): 20sec

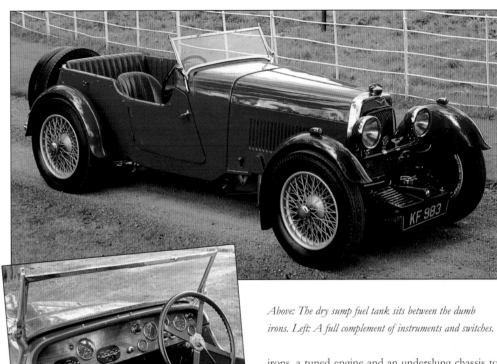

Above: The dry sump fuel tank sits between the dumb irons. Left: A full complement of instruments and switches.

they were buying little more than the name, Renwick and Bertelli, together with father and son Charnwood, formed Aston Martin Motors in October 1926. They acquired new premises in Feltham and set up a proper machine shop with production facilities and a body-making shop run by Enrico Bertelli.

The all-new car, using the Claude Hill engine, was first seen at the London Motor Show in 1927. There were two basic models, the T-series with a long chassis for the saloon and tourer and the S-series, the sporting model with a chassis which was lower and a foot shorter. The transmission used a separate gearbox and a worm-drive rear axle with most of the components made at Feltham. The 1494cc engine gave 56bhp at 4250rpm which was enough to power a sports model to 80mph (129km/h). The chassis followed normal practice with semi-elliptic leaf springs, Perrot brakes and Hartford shock absorbers.

Left: The Series One had the new overhead camshaft engine and came in two chassis versions. The shorter, lower chassis was used for this 1930 International 2/4 seater.

With the new model under way, Bertelli also wanted to take Aston Martin into racing and to the Le Mans 24 hour race in particular. So for 1928 they built the first of the LM series, a designation which was to denote the factory racers throughout the 'thirties. LM1 and LM2 used a revised 'dry-sump' oil system with its tank sitting between the front dumb-

irons, a tuned engine and an underslung chassis to make them lower. They didn't fare well at Le Mans, but the dry-sump engine was introduced for production in the International model in 1929 and a tuned UIster version of the engine became available in 1930 for an extra £50 – racing was already improving the breed.

The International was offered in two- and four-seater forms on the same 8ft 6in (2591mm) (short) chassis at £598 for 1929. With their low build, mudguards attached to the brake back-plates and thus moving with the wheels, the International was one of the most effective sports cars available.

Production dates 1926-32

11

Aston Martin Le Mans & Series Two

DESPITE the fact that Aston Martin was making a good sporting name for itself, it was still not making money and the company continued to spend too much on racing even though it was an effective development medium. The Charnwoods withdrew first, followed by Renwick, leaving Bertelli on his own. He brought in new money from Aston dealers and friends, reforming the company as Aston Martin Limited in 1929, just as the Depression set in. By 1931 they

needed further help which came from the owner of Frazer Nash, H.J. Aldington who took charge of sales. But by the end of the year, Bertelli had persuaded London dealer Lance Prideaux-Brune to invest and so regain Aston's independence.

It was he who was responsible for the Second Series of the 1.5-litre cars after around 130 of the First Series cars had been produced over the previous five years. Production costs had to be reduced to enable Aston Martin to drop prices to a

level that the post-depression market could afford. It was the start of the philosophy that has helped so many small-volume makers over the years – if the eye cannot see it, replace it with proprietary components. Instead of making their own, Aston Martin bought in Laycock gearboxes mounted directly to the engine, and ENV spiral-bevel back-axle gearing.

Below: Low and lithe, a 1933 Le Mans 2/4 seater.

Underneath, it was a new if similar chassis too, easier to make and with cable-operated front brakes instead of the Perrrot-shaft system. The torque tube between gearbox and back axle was also removed. The New International was launched in February 1932 using the previous coachwork styles on long and short chassis with the price now reduced to £475; the engine was now producing 60bhp at 4500rpm on a 6.5:1 compression ratio. The long-chassis tourer was known as the Standard or 12/50 model.

Only a dozen New Internationals were sold before a Le Mans model superseded it. A few replicas of the works Series One racers had been built in 1931 and sold as Le Mans models. The new 85mph (137km/h) Le Mans had a much lower radiator line than the New International and a 70bhp engine; it would be offered initially as a two-seater with a slab-tank tail, then a 2/4-seater, as this example (BOW 73) and a long-chassis four-seater. Later models would have 18-inch wheels rather than the previous 21-inch wheels. The Standard chassis continued for Tourers and Saloons with the less powerful engine.

Prideaux-Brune's finances had been well-stretched during 1932 and he returned to his dealer role, but a new fairy godmother had arrived in the form of Sir Arthur Sutherland, a Newcastle shipping magnate, who placed his son Gordon alongside Bertelli as Joint MD. Gordon Sutherland had had a formal automobile engineering training through Alvis and the Chelsea Automobile Engineering College, but he looked after the sales and service side leaving Bertelli as Technical Director. It was the Sutherland influence that was to

bring in the Le Mans model after the New International's slow start. 130 models had been built by the time the third 1.5-litre variant arrived at the beginning of 1934 – the Mk II.

Above: This Competition 2-seater had a body from one of the works racers and was built for R.O. Shuttleworth who raced in many events. Below: The sohc engine is cleanly styled; note the aluminium casting for the bulkhead.

Production dates   1932-33

SPECIFICATION	1933 LE MANS
ENGINE	4-cylinder sohc, 1494cc
HORSEPOWER	70bhp @ 4750rpm
TRANSMISSION	4-speed manual
CHASSIS	Steel channel, aluminium body
SUSPENSION	Beam/live axle on leaf springs
BRAKES	4-wheel drum brakes
TOP SPEED	82mph (132km/h)
ACCELERATION	0-50mph (80km/h): 16sec

Aston Martin Mark II

WHILE Bertelli was happy to concentrate on engineering the sports and competition cars, the Sutherlands worked to add refinement to the new model. Passengers needed to be better insulated from the road and from engine vibrations and noise. The new chassis gained strength and stiffness by making the channel section of the two side-frame members somewhat deeper in the middle, while an extra cross-member was added and the cast aluminium bulkhead structure was enlarged.

To improve roadholding, the twin Hartford friction shock absorbers at the front were turned through 90 degrees so that the moving arms could act directly on the wheel upright – the extreme end of the axle. The theoretical improvement in wheel control would have been even greater if the unsprung weight had been reduced by removing the cycle wing mounting from the brake backplate; even the saloons maintained this feature, but it has to be admitted that close-fitting cycle wings keep the frontal area down, which is good for maximum speed. The powerful brakes were still operated by cables; Aston Martin braking was extremely good thanks to large Alfin drums that virtually filled the 18-inch wheels.

The engine was reworked with a stiffer, fully counterbalanced crankshaft carrying wider timing gears, and a modified cylinder head increased the power to 73bhp at 5200rpm; revised Silentbloc mounting bushes and a new cam-chain tensioner contributed to improved refinement. The most obvious external difference was the thermostatically controlled radiator shutters replacing the wire mesh that had served for so long.

SPECIFICATION	1934 MARK II
ENGINE	4-cylinder sohc, 1494cc
HORSEPOWER	73bhp @ 4750rpm
TRANSMISSION	4-speed manual
CHASSIS	Steel channel, aluminium body
SUSPENSION	Beam/live axle on leaf springs
BRAKES	4-wheel drum brakes
TOP SPEED	84mph (135km/h)
ACCELERATION	0-50mph (80km/h): 15sec

The Mark II came in two chassis lengths as before but the long chassis had a 10 ft (3048mm) wheelbase to provide full four-seater accommodation in the graceful saloons and drophead coupés like the one illustrated. While such a wheelbase seems exceptionally long for a 1.5-litre car, the purpose was to ensure that rear passengers could be placed ahead of the rear axle and thus allow a lower roofline. The resultant wheel-at-each-corner look contributed much to the lasting elegance.

The *Autocar* tested the 2/4-seater, four-seater and saloon versions recording maximum speeds of 85mph (137km/h) with the screen folded flat, 81mph (130km/h) and 76mph (122km/h) respectively. They were impressed by the overall integrity of each one – 'it is a combination of features which puts the Aston where it is among the world's finer high performance cars . . . each feature which a really good high performance car must have

Left: The Mark II came in a variety of styles. The long wheelbase allowed rear passengers to sit low thus keeping overall height down on this 1934 saloon. As with the previous Bertelli cars, front wings turned with the wheels.

is right and the merging of them results in something exceptional . . .' these comments referred to the long-wheelbase four-seater.

Like its predecessor, the Mk II only lasted two years before the next model, but 166 examples were made between January 1934 and December 1935. This figure includes some 20 Ulsters, the competition two-seater recalled on the next pages.

Production dates	1934-35

Right: The drophead coupé, a 1935 example here, gave good protection when the hood was raised and taller doors kept some of the draught out. Below: This 1934 2/4-seater Tourer is more spartan and certainly sportier.

15

Aston Martin Ulster

BASED on the Mk II chassis, the Ulster was the apotheosis of the pre-war sporting Aston Martins. A replica of the 1934 team cars which had finished 3rd, 6th and 7th in the Ulster TT race, it was made available to amateur racers for just £750. The engine was tuned with a 9.5:1 compression ratio, big carburettors and polished ports to give 80bhp at 5250rpm, which was enough to push the low sleek car to the 100mph (161km/h) guaranteed in the brochure. A full length undertray helped to keep the aerodynamic drag down and the frontal area was as low as possible.

Right: LM18 was a 1935 works car; Bertelli chose Italian red for better luck than experienced with British racing green

It certainly looked the part with the narrow body permitted by race regulations, and a curvy boat tail shaped to carry the spare wheel flat on the floor. A racing exhaust system ran along the left side of the car through a Brooklands silencer and out through a fishtail – although few have these now; passengers had to be careful to avoid the hot exhaust system when getting out. The car came with a fold-flat windscreen and a pair of aero-screens which could be used singly for competition.

The cockpit was a fighter pilot's delight with a row of identical aircraft switches neatly labelled on the passenger's side. The passenger also had the clock, leaving the essential instruments to the driver. A big lever on the steering wheel controlled the ignition advance/retard which was a sensitive business with such a high compression ratio.

The three cars built for the 1934 Le Mans were LM11, LM12 and LM14. The French race allowed cars to be lightened, so all had their frames drilled to remove surplus metal. In fact all three retired from the race with silly mechanical problems. The Tourist Trophy regulations decreed standard chassis, so LM11 and LM12 were given new frames and rechristened LM15 and LM16, to which was added LM17 to make a team of three. Until this point all the works Astons had run in variations of British racing green; convinced that something was needed to overcome the bad luck at Le Mans, Bertelli had the TT cars painted his Italian red. It worked. Not only did they all finish well but Aston Martin won the Team Prize and earned the name that was given to the replicas that would be sold.

Further improvements were made to the design for 1935 and three new Italian red cars were built, LM18, LM19 and LM20. Engine power was increased to 85bhp and the cars had lower radiators which led to sloping rather than strictly horizontal bonnets. LM20 took a remarkable third place overall, LM18 was 12th and LM19 crashed. Returning to Ulster with four cars – LM21 was added – the Team Prize was taken again with 4th, 5th and 11th.

Of the 166 Mark IIs, 21 were Ulsters and four of these had 2/4-seater bodywork. So the true

Above: The Ulster's shapely tail hides a horizontal spare wheel – 1934 here. Right: Speedometers are for passengers.

SPECIFICATION	1935 ULSTER
ENGINE	4-cylinder sohc, 1494cc
HORSEPOWER	85bhp @ 5250rpm
TRANSMISSION	4-speed manual
CHASSIS	Steel channel, aluminium body
SUSPENSION	Beam/live axles on leaf springs
BRAKES	4-wheel drum brakes
TOP SPEED	100mph (161km/h)
ACCELERATION	50mph (0-80km/h): 12sec

Ulster is a rare car but one of the best that Aston Martin made pre-war. It was also the last of the 1.5-litre Bertelli cars.

Production dates 1934-35

Aston Martin 15/98 2-litre

BY THE end of 1935, the Bertelli Aston Martins had established a good reputation as sporting cars that could easily be used for competition, or apparently more touring versions which had full-blown coachwork on longer versions of the sports chassis. The Sutherlands felt that the 2/4- and four-seater cars should be designed to provide real comfort rather than just space, so the 15/98 was evolved accordingly – 15 RAC-rated horsepower and 98 real bhp – with a larger version of the Bertelli/Hill engine.

Rumours of an impending 2-litre engine in early 1936 were finally confirmed when the works entries for the Le Mans 24 hours were published. The factory entered three 1.5-litre Ulsters to defend their previous class win and two new cars. These had more or less the same chassis as the Ulster, and the same wheelbase but a little wider and stiffer, but the beam front axle had an upper cable location to prevent spring wind-up with the new powerful Lockheed hydraulic brakes. And finally the front wings were chassis-mounted but braced with wire stays.

The new engine had somewhat less revvable dimensions with 78 x 102mm (3 x 4in) dimensions – against the 1.56-litre's 69.3 x 99mm (2.7 x 3.9in) – to give all but 1950cc. For these Le Mans cars, the

Below: This 1936 2-litre Speed Model was originally fitted with this Ulster-style body. Jock Horsfall raced it before the last war and went on to win the 1946 Belgian GP in it.

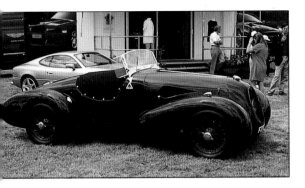

Above: The 2-litre Speed Model's C-Type body was an interesting exercise in aerodynamics, if not style.

Above: With the 2-litre, moving mudguards disappeared. This full 4-door coachwork was a lot of weight for a 2-litre engine.

output was 'well over 100bhp'. Unfortunately Le Mans was cancelled that year due to French strikes and these cars were sold to privateers; however two replicas – Speed Models – were built for other privateers and these contested the 1936 TT, with Dick Seaman leading the class rival BMW 328s until a main bearing finally went. The two Le Mans cars were the last works cars that the factory built before the war; they obviously contained a lot of Bertelli influence but that was his final input. The

SPECIFICATION	1938 15/98 DHC
ENGINE	4-cylinder sohc, 1950cc
HORSEPOWER	98bhp @ 5000rpm
TRANSMISSION	4-speed manual
CHASSIS	Steel channel, aluminium body
SUSPENSION	Beam/live axles on leaf springs
BRAKES	4-wheel hydraulic drum brakes
TOP SPEED	85mph (137km/h)
ACCELERATION	0-50mph (80km/h): 14sec

Sutherlands felt less strongly about race-proving and Bertelli resigned that year; nevertheless, he had earned his place in Aston Martin lore.

A few more of the Speed Models were built with two- and 2/4-seater bodywork before the final few were clad in a 'streamlined' body as the C-Type – not beautiful and no faster!

The roadgoing 15/98 was to be the mainstay, available in a variety of body forms, but with a wet-sump version of the engine producing 98bhp, which was enough to propel the sports tourers to around 85mph (137km/h). The chassis was similar to that of the Le Mans cars but available in 8ft 3in (2515mm) and 9ft 6in (2896mm) forms; E. Bertelli built most of the early bodies, and particularly the

saloons, until his brother's resignation from the company, but Abbotts and Abbey shared the rest. All had chassis-mounted wings which made them somewhat less distinctive than the Mk IIs had been. Prices in 1937 ranged from £575 to £625 for the saloons and tourers (reduced by £100 for the following year) to the Speed Model's £775.

As the Feltham company moved towards the war period, they had built another 173 cars over the four years from July 1936 and their reputation had moved away from the sports car to the fast tourer. However the total Bertelli/Sutherland production was just 618 cars over 12.5 years – about one a week.

Production dates	1936-39

Left: This 1938 2/4-seater tourer used the short chassis with Abbey bodywork and was originally a works demonstration model. With its sloping radiator and elegant wings it looked the sporting part, while the running board gave easy access and kept mud away from passengers' sleeves. With 98bhp available from the wet-sump 2-litre engine, the sports cars were capable of over 85mph (137km/h). As ever it was fully instrumented for the sporting driver.

Aston Martin Atom

THERE IS only one Atom and it well demonstrates the engineering talents of Gordon Sutherland and Claude Hill. Once the 15/98 series was under way and production was proceeding at a reasonable rate, the two directed their thoughts to the future. A special 'air-line' saloon known as Donald Duck had been built in 1938 using 15/98 components; it was the first step towards the all-new car that Sutherland and Hill were planning. The open two-seater C-Type Speed Model came next, rather smoother in line. And by mid-1939 they had built the prototype of what

might have been their next model had not war intervened; it was a far-sighted project embodying many new principles and partners.

The chassis of this new Atom used air-frame principles with a superstructure welded on top of basic longerons; it was made up of square section tubing – readily available and easier to weld together than round tube – and was deeper at floor level, and lighter for the upper levels which added stiffness and gave the basic body outline. The aluminium body panels were wrapped round or screwed to the frame; while this practice had been used by the

Italian coachbuilder Touring and by Hill on Donald Duck, the Atom's use of the body tubes as an integral part of the chassis was original thinking.

The body that it carried certainly seemed aerodynamic but any style was limited by the square tubing, and flat glass which meant a windscreen in two parts. In outline it was very much like a C-Type with a close-coupled four-door saloon section squeezed into the middle, the doors being hinged off the central pillar. Where the C-Type buried its headlights behind a large wire-mesh grille, the Atom had near-flush lights within the full-width front panel which had lost any separate definition of the wings. No grille, just a few slats in a triangular form. It was a striking shape which was to remain 'advanced' for many years.

The suspension too had much of interest. Independent front suspension was used by some manufacturers but it was rare. The Atom used a system patented by Gordon Armstrong. This employed a large cast trailing arm which held the stub axle; above this, with its lever arm parallel, was a hydraulic damper. A coil spring acting on the stub-axle provided the actual springing, also very unusual for the period, while the steering linkage used a divided track rod to minimize any bump steering effect. The rear suspension, however, just used leaf springs, but the axle itself showed a very early use of the Salisbury hypoid bevel rear axle which allowed a lower prop-shaft line than usual.

Left: The unique Atom was Gordon Sutherland's mobile testbed for the post-war models. Designed by Claude Hill it featured many novel features, including the space-frame superstructure and Armstrong independent front springing.

SPECIFICATION	1944 ATOM
ENGINE	4-cylinder pushrod ohv, 1970cc
HORSEPOWER	80bhp @ 4750rpm (6:1 CR)
TRANSMISSION	4-speed Cotal Electric control
CHASSIS	Square-section tubular frame, aluminium body
SUSPENSION	Trailing arm, live rear axle on leaf springs
BRAKES	4-wheel hydraulic drum brakes
TOP SPEED	105mph (169km/h)
ACCELERATION	0-60mph (96km/h): 18sec

The Atom was planned to have Claude Hill's new 2-litre, push-rod, overhead-valve engine but war-time work delayed that until 1944, so early development was completed with a 15/98 engine. However, this still used the Cotal electric gearbox, a 4-speed epicyclic unit with selection controlled by solenoids operated by a minute gear-lever mounted on the dashboard. The 2-litre engine is part of the next model story.

There was much that was novel on the Atom and everyone who drove it during the war years was very impressed, convinced that they had driven the

Above: Advanced in shape and under the skin, the Atom carried no obvious clue to its Aston design. The close coupled doors were in response to a proposed new racing regulation.

car of the future. Even now its ride comfort is remarkably good. It served its purpose in convincing David Brown that Aston Martin was worth buying, a fact which allowed many of its features to be incorporated into the new models. It has now been restored to its 1946 specification.

Production dates	Only one built – 1939-46

Aston Martin 2-litre Sports

COME THE end of the war, which had seen the company working for the Ministry of Aircraft Production, and Aston Martin needed to return to motoring production, but the Atom was not a commercial proposition and money was required to create a derivative that would have market appeal. Gordon Sutherland decided to advertise the company for sale. One person who saw it was David Brown, the industrialist, who drove the Atom and was sufficiently impressed to buy the company, retaining Claude Hill and Gordon Sutherland. By this time, of course, the Atom had Claude Hill's new pushrod 4-cylinder engine.

Brown had driven sporting Astons before and decided that a sports version of the Atom would be his first car, which was to become the DB1. The chassis, longer by 6in (152mm), followed the square-tube space-frame concept but the side members were twin-tubes and smaller tubes made up a scuttle. The front suspension was improved by joining the pivots of the two trailing arms with a transverse torsion anti-roll bar, which showed a very early appreciation of suspension theory. The rear axle was better located using substantial trailing arms with coil springs atop and a Panhard rod; Armstrong dampers were mounted on the axle. The gearbox was changed too, to use a David Brown 4-speed unit. But the rest of the new DB1 was very much Atom-inspired – the thousands of miles that Sutherland had covered during the war had proved that everything worked.

Below: Known in retrospect as the DB1, Aston Martin's new post-war car was launched as the 2-litre Sports.

*The 90bhp pushrod
2-litre gave over
90mph (145km/h)*

styling was not the most attractive but it established the post-war face of the Aston Martin grille, a tall centre section flanked by lower sides. It was a lot of car for a 2-litre to carry around and the £1498 list price put it into a much higher purchase tax bracket than the new Jaguar XK 120 which cost £988.

As convinced as the pre-war owners that racing improved and promoted the breed, David Brown announced in March 1949 that Aston Martin would be at Le Mans that year with three closed coupés, two with the Hill 4-cylinder, and one with a twin-cam six-cylinder engine. While Claude Hill had been working on a six-cylinder version of his own engine, David Brown chose to buy Lagonda instead and take advantage of the new 2.6-litre engine for the next generation of Aston Martins. Claude Hill resigned a little later. One of the 2-litre cars finished in 7th place that year; the 'six' lost its water but redeemed itself by finishing 3rd in the Spa 24-hours – the DB2 was on the way and the 2-litre Sports became the DB1.

The new engine had been designed for ease of production and serviceability without loss of sporting performance. The side-mounted camshaft was chain-driven from the rear of the crankshaft and operated overhead valve gear through push-rods and rockers; the inlet valves sat vertically but the exhaust valves were angled away to lead the ports into a finned cast manifold via a horizontal face on top of the cylinder head. It was an unusual treatment but period thinking believed that the secret of performance was to improve exhaust flow which would consequently suck in more mixture. The crankshaft had five main bearings with a wet-sump oil system; all the oil passages were internal

drillings rather than pipework. With dimensions of 82.55 x 92mm (3.25 x 3.6in) (1970cc), the engine was smoother and more free-revving than the pre-war units and gave 90bhp at 4750rpm.

The mechanical details of the cars were announced in March 1948, and DB1 prototypes were running during the summer of 1948 including one that was converted into a lightweight two-seater with which Jock Horsfall and Leslie Johnson won the Spa 24-hour race. When the cars were shown in the autumn of 1948, a Spa replica was offered but it attracted no takers in the depressed market of the time. The regular open sports car fared little better and only 15 were sold by the end of 1950. Its body

Production dates	1948-50

SPECIFICATION	1948 2-LITRE SPORTS
ENGINE	4-cylinder pushrod ohv, 1970cc
HORSEPOWER	90bhp @ 4750rpm (7.25:1 CR)
TRANSMISSION	4-speed manual DB
CHASSIS	Square-section tube frame
SUSPENSION	Trailing arm, live rear axle on coil springs
BRAKES	4-wheel hydraulic drum brakes
TOP SPEED	93mph (150km/h)
ACCELERATION	0-60mph (96km/h): 14sec

Aston Martin DB2

THE 1949 Le Mans coupés based on the DB1 chassis can be regarded as prototypes for the DB2 which was announced in April 1950. Their bodies had been designed by Frank Feeley, who had come to Aston Martin via Lagonda, and were arguably the first of the English GT cars – the Italian Gran Turismo style set the trend of high speed comfort for two under a fast-back saloon roof. It was a very clean design and the complete front bodywork hinged forward to give easy access to the engine compartment.

The DB2 followed the DB1 chassis design fairly closely but was 9in (229mm) shorter in the wheelbase; square tubes were still used with outriggers and tubular formers on which to hang the aluminium body. The rear suspension now used twin trailing arms each side, retaining the Panhard rod and coil springs.

It was an exciting specification for the period, made more so by the new 2.6-litre twin-cam six. This had been designed by Willie Watson under W.O. Bentley who had moved to Lagonda following

the Rolls-Royce take-over of Bentley Motors. With 3 x 3.5in (78 x 90mm) dimensions it was still 'under-square' but, as launched in 1950, it developed 105bhp at 5000rpm; racing developments allowed a 'high performance' Vantage version to be offered at the end of the year with 125bhp, by which time a convertible was also in the range.

The 1950 racing programme had been master-minded by John Wyer who was to become a significant Aston Martin figure over the next 12 years. Le Mans saw them 5th and 6th overall (1st and 2nd in the 3-litre class); the Silverstone 1-hour Production Car race saw three finishing 10th, 12th and 15th (2nd, 3rd and 4th in the 3-litre class behind Duncan Hamilton's Healey) and the year finished with the TT where they were 4th and 5th with a 1, 2, 3 in the class.

By the end of the year the grille had lost the divisions between the centre and side sections, and attained the familiar shape that has stayed with us with subtle alterations over the years. The 1951 models thus embodied the definitive DB2 shape which would see 411 models, including 100 or so convertibles, produced over the three-year period. Le Mans that year produced the DB2's best results; with 138bhp and much lightened chassis, the three entries finished 3rd, 5th and 7th.

With the DB2, Aston Martin had moved into the upper league of sporting machinery and now had the performance to match the high price that was very much a function of the small-volume,

Left: This early DB2 was used in 1950 as the development car for the Lagonda 2.6-litre engine and was the sixth to be built. Front and side grilles were to disappear in production.

SPECIFICATION	1950 DB2
ENGINE	6-cylinder dohc, 2580cc
HORSEPOWER	105bhp @ 5000rpm
TRANSMISSION	4-speed manual DB
CHASSIS	Square-section tube frame, aluminium body
SUSPENSION	Trailing arm, live rear axle on coil springs
BRAKES	4-wheel hydraulic drum brakes
TOP SPEED	110mph (177km/h)
ACCELERATION	0-60mph (96km/h): 12.4sec 0-100mph (161km/h): 38.8sec

By 1952 the DB2 had become defined; the screen was still a two-piece affair but the grille set the pattern for the future.

27

hand-built production methods. Including purchase tax, the 1952 DB2 cost £2724 and the convertible £2879, while the Jaguar XK 120 coupé was just £1694.

Motor magazine tested a DB2 in 1953, by which time all used the 125bhp engine; they recorded a maximum speed of 117mph (188km/h) with 0-60mph (0-96km/h) in 11.2 seconds and the standing start quarter mile in 18.5 seconds. The DB2 had come a long way from Claude Hill's Atom, but without it, Aston Martin would not have found a saviour in David Brown, and he would not have been able to get production under way so soon.

Production dates 1950-53

Aston Martin DB2/4

WHILE the DB2 was a true Grand Tourer for two in the best continental tradition, there was obviously a market for the couple who had children in the period before the family needed a true four-seater saloon. The DB2 had a large luggage platform, so a little chassis surgery made space above the rear axle for two small seats and a slight increase in headroom did not detract from the GT lines despite a 7in (178mm) increase in overall length.

With the luggage now carried further back, the DB2/4 needed rear access and thus became one of the first ever production cars with an opening rear door contained in normal bodywork, as opposed to an estate car. Just like any modern hatchback, the small rear seat backs folded down to increase flat floor space.

As before there were just the two styles, saloon and drophead coupé, the latter accounting for some 70 of the 565 cars made in the two years from the October 1953 Motor Show launch. A feature that instantly modernized the appearance was the arrival of the full-width screen.

Autocar was quick to publish a test of the new car, still with the 125bhp engine, and it was duly impressed. The extra height and weight had decreased the maximum speed from 117mph to 111mph (188 to 179km/h) and increased the 0-60mph (0-96km/h) time from 11.2 to 12.6 seconds, but it was still a high performance car and could carry two adults and two children. They commented

that the fuel consumption was good for such performance, giving over 20mpg (14 litres/100km) to give a continental driving range of over 300 miles (480km) from the 17-gallon (77-litre) tank.

The suspension could cope well with all standards of road with excellent stability, good handling and a ride quality that surprised all. There was little road or wind noise, although engine and gearbox were audible. The driving position could be

Below: As the name implies, the DB2/4 was a 2+2. The opening rear window anticipated the hatchbacks of the future.

SPECIFICATION	1953 DB2/4
ENGINE	6-cylinder dohc, 2580cc
HORSEPOWER	125bhp @ 5000rpm
TRANSMISSION	4-speed manual DB
CHASSIS	Square-section tube frame, aluminium body
SUSPENSION	Trailing arm, live axle on coil springs
BRAKES	4-wheel hydraulic drum brakes
TOP SPEED	114mph (183km/h)
ACCELERATION	0-60mph (96km/h): 12.6sec 0-100mph (161km/h): 40.4sec

tailored to all sizes with the normal fore and aft adjustment complemented by a telescopic steering column and an adjustable seat backrest. As with all previous Astons, there was a full range of instrumentation laid out on the wooden dashboard.

Autocar concluded with the comments . . .

'The Aston Martin DB2-4 is a sports car with a very definite appeal. It has full saloon car comfort, coupled with performance and roadholding of a very high order, yet in spite of its very good performance the fuel consumption was not excessive.'

Above: The 2/4 was also offered as a drophead coupé. The 2/4 is recognizable from its predecessor by the full-width screen. Full instrumentation remained an Aston feature.

In the middle of 1954 the engine was enlarged to 3-litres by increasing the bore size from 78 to 83mm (3 to 3.25in). This boosted the power to 140bhp at 5000rpm, enough to put the performance back to DB2 levels.

By this time Aston Martin were engaged in International sports car racing with the purpose-built DB3 and DB3S models, so the DB2/4 was not raced by the factory, although two cars ran in the 1955 Mille Miglia with 170bhp engines. They suffered clutch failures; three cars had been used earlier in the Monte Carlo Rally – they won the team prize.

Production dates	1953-55

29

Aston Martin DB2/4 Mark II

THERE was not a lot of difference between the Mk II and its predecessor; a few details changed that were just enough to justify calling it a new model. A little more headroom was created in the rear, the tail had little fins to appeal to the American market which expected them, and that part of the bonnet behind the wheel arch was now fixed, lessening the effort needed to lift the bonnet usefully. Inside, the seats had more side support, and the handbrake reverted to the pre-war fly-off type which was very much easier to use for hill starts.

There was, however, a new body style in addition to the saloon and drophead coupé. This was a fixed-head coupé which gave it the same profile as the drophead; it was a notchback with a separate boot, rather than a fastback. Of the 199 Mk IIs, 34 were fixed-head coupés and around 24 drophead coupés.

Until the arrival of the DB2/4, Aston Martins were assembled at Feltham. Engines, chassis and gearboxes were made at another David Brown factory in Farsley near Leeds, arriving at Feltham

where the bodies were made and fitted. Lagondas were also assembled in Feltham using bodies made by Tickford in Newport Pagnell. In 1954, David Brown bought Tickford with a view to moving all production out of Feltham. Lagonda and Aston Martin assembly then moved to a David Brown factory in Huddersfield, with the Lagondas still

Below: Only three of the new DB2/4 Mk II chassis were fitted with this low, sleek bodywork which was designed and built by Touring of Milan, who would later shape the DB4.

30

SPECIFICATION	1956 DB2/4 Mk II Spyder
ENGINE	6-cylinder dohc, 2922cc
HORSEPOWER	140bhp @ 5000rpm
TRANSMISSION	4-speed manual DB
CHASSIS	Square-section tube frame, aluminium body
SUSPENSION	Trailing arm, live axle on coil springs
BRAKES	4-wheel hydraulic drum
TOP SPEED	120mph (193km/h)
ACCELERATION	0-60mph (96km/h): 9.5sec 0-100mph (161km/h): 26.0sec

using Tickford bodies and Astons having bodies built by Mulliner. This allowed Feltham to remain the centre for service, engineering development and the race team. With the arrival of the Aston 2/4 Mk II all the standard Aston bodies were made by Tickford. During the lifetime of the Mk II, all Aston assembly work would be concentrated in Newport Pagnell.

However a trio of DB2/4 Mk II chassis were sent out to the Italian coachbuilder Touring based in Milan. Touring was founded in 1926 but had made a particular name for itself in the late 'thirties with its Superleggera (super-light) body construction. This was used by various Italian sports car manufacturers as well as for a special series of BMW 328; aluminum bodywork was wrapped round steel tubes welded to the main chassis, a principle similar to that adopted on the Atom. It was simple and light.

Touring also had a good styling department and came up with a most attractive two-seater Spyder. The one shown here was the first to be built

Above and right: This car was the first of the three and was offered as the prize in a 1956 Daily Mail *competition.*

and was offered as a prize by the *Daily Mail* at the time of the 1956 Motor Show. The third one was also exhibited there, while the second one was at the Paris salon. While Touring would have liked to have continued with a limited production run, no orders were forthcoming, but the association was nevertheless to be a useful one.

Production dates 1955-57

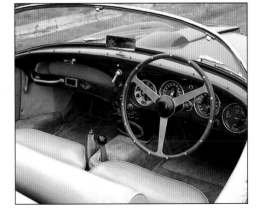

Aston Martin DB Mark III

THE LAST of the Atom-based cars was launched at the Geneva Show in March 1957. It is logical enough to call it the DB2/4 Mk III but somehow the 2/4 bit was dropped and it has always been known as the Mk III, not to be confused with the earlier sports-racing DB3 and DB3S. The basic chassis and body design was carried over from its predecessor but the revised grille shape – an echo of the DB3S – was a worthwhile improvement.

The major change was to the engine. Tadek Marek, an expatriate Pole, had been brought in from Austin as an Engine Designer in 1954 to start work on the new DB4 engine, but first he almost completely redesigned the existing engine, which was given a new type number – DBA. New block assembly, new crankshaft, new camshafts, new manifolds all contributed to give 162bhp at 5500rpm from the existing 2922cc. Various engine options came as a result of the sports car racing programme; the DBB included triple Weber carburettors, high-lift cams, higher compression and a claim of 195bhp.

Girling disc front brakes were initially an option but became standard after the first 100 (out of 550) had been produced. The increasing option list included an overdrive from 1958 at £105 and automatic transmission from 1959 at £150. Given the car price of £3450, including tax, the cost of extras was quite reasonable.

There were other detail changes too. Previous instruments were grouped around the centre of the fascia, but the Mk III incorporated them all into a hooded binnacle behind the steering wheel, a feature that would be retained through to the DB6. And the rear quarter lights were hinged. Of the 550 cars, 350 went to the USA. Most of the production were the saloons, but there were 85 drophead coupés and a handful of the notchback fixed-head coupés.

Autocar's test of a saloon with the standard 162bhp engine showed the car to be usefully faster despite the extra weight of increased comfort – 3000lb or nearly 1340kg. Maximum speed was up to

Left and above: A DB3S-style grille, front disc brakes and a more powerful engine were the main features of the last of the DB2 series. This instrument binnacle was also new.

SPECIFICATION	1957 DB Mk III Saloon
ENGINE	6-cylinder dohc, 2922cc
HORSEPOWER	162bhp @ 5500rpm
TRANSMISSION	4-speed manual DB
CHASSIS	Square-section tube frame, aluminium body
SUSPENSION	Trailing arm, live axle on coil springs
BRAKES	Servo-assisted disc front/ drum rear
TOP SPEED	119mph (192km/h)
ACCELERATION	0-60mph (96km/h): 9.3sec 0-100mph (161km/h): 31.0sec

Above: With 162bhp from the revised engine, the DB Mark III was capable of nearly 120mph (193km/h); it was still using many features developed on the Atom.

119mph (192km/h) in direct top or overdrive, with 0-60mph (0-96km/h) coming up in 9.3 seconds and a standing start quarter mile covered in 17.4 seconds; at last, a DB2/4 that was faster than the original DB2 which was some 500lb (227kg) lighter.

While the DB Mk III theoretically overlapped with the start of DB4 production, the reality was that the DB4 was not ready for production when it was first shown in October 1958, so the Mk III had to continue for longer than originally planned. Fortunately it was a very good car and the saloon was also £900 cheaper than the £4000 DB4.

With the phasing out of the DB Mk III in 1959 went the last connection with the pioneering work of Claude Hill 20 years earlier.

Production dates 1957-59

Aston Martin DB4

WITH THE arrival of the DB4 Britain finally had a GT that could take on the best of the Continental specialists. It had safe 140mph (225km/h) performance and the looks to go with it, thanks to coachbuilders Touring; those DB2/4 Spyders were a prelude to greater things. And it was a reasonable four-seater too.

Work had started on the DB2/4 replacement back in 1954 and Harold Beach had been assigned the task of chassis design and development. The first prototype used a perimeter frame which carried wishbone front suspension and a de Dion axle;

using a 3-litre engine, it was clad in a sort of DB2 body and did many development miles. John Wyer, then Technical Director, wanted to use Touring both for their style and their method of construction. When Harold Beach took his prototype to Milan, they insisted on a platform chassis as the basis for their tubular superstructure. Beach redesigned the chassis, retaining his wishbone and de Dion suspensions.

Tadek Marek had started on the engine a year later. Wyer wanted an all-aluminium, 3-litre 'six' that could be stretched to 3.5-litres. Marek wanted to

design it for familiar cast iron and he did not want to get involved in racing, so he aimed for a less stressed 3.7-litre. It was a classic twin-cam six with seven main bearings and 'square' 92 x 92mm (3.6 x 3.6in) dimensions. Come the time for casting the first blocks, however, and Aston could not find an iron foundry to take it on; only an aluminium foundry would help which meant a minor redesign to take removable wet liners. So the engine perforce became an all-aluminium unit, and it would race with great success in the DBR2 before it was even in production for the DB4. With twin SU carburettors it produced a claimed net power of 240bhp at 5500rpm.

Below: Only 70 convertibles were built out of 1110 DB4s.

Left: The author admires the 3.7-litre aluminium twin-cam six that Tadek Marek designed for the DB4.

had Dunlop disc brakes all round, this was easily accomplished. The average of the two magazines' top speeds was almost exactly 140mph (225km/h). It was a very impressive car and put Aston Martin back in the forefront of sporting manufacturers.

Over the years to 1963 there would be five minor series which gave something fresh to sell at each Motor Show, some with more significant changes than others. Overdrive became an option in 1960 for the Series 2. A Vantage option with an extra 25bhp came with the Series 4. Convertibles joined the range in 1961 but only 70 were made out of the total 1110 DB4s built.

SPECIFICATION	1961 DB4
ENGINE	6-cylinder dohc, 3670cc
HORSEPOWER	220bhp (net) @ 5500rpm
TRANSMISSION	4-speed manual DB
CHASSIS	Steel sheet with tubular frame for aluminium body
SUSPENSION	Wishbone, live axle on coil springs
BRAKES	Servo-assisted disc
TOP SPEED	140mph (225km/h)
ACCELERATION	0-60mph (96km/h): 8.9sec 0-100mph (161km/h): 20.9sec

Production dates 1958-63

The new engine was mated to a David Brown gearbox but the final drive system lost its de Dion axle in favour of a live axle located by twin radius arms and a transverse Watt linkage. The new chassis was clean and simple using flat sheet metal welded up in substantial jigs at Farsley. These were sent to Newport Pagnell for the *Superleggera* superstructure to be welded on and the aluminium panels to be wrapped around the tubes.

The DB4 was far from ready for production, however, and a vehicle builders strike gave the engineering department useful time to continue development. It was to be nearly two years after the launch that *Autocar* and *Motor* had the chance to assess performance figures and prove the advertising claim that the DB4 was the first car to be capable of 0-100-0mph (0-161-0km/h) in under 30 seconds; as it could reach 100mph (161km/h) in 21 seconds and

Below: Although it was styled by Italian coachbuilder Touring, who also licensed its Superleggera body frame construction, the DB4 established Aston Martin as makers of the English Grand Tourer. This example is one of the final series which ran from September 1962 to June 1963.

35

Aston Martin DB4GT & GT Zagato

ALL PREVIOUS production Aston Martins had racing derivatives and the DB4 was to be no exception; it was in the company's blood. In early 1959, when the standard DB4 had only been launched a few months, and development was still ongoing, the engineers built an experimental short wheelbase version.

Five inches (127mm) were chopped out of the wheelbase, the rear seats were deleted in favour of a luggage platform and generally lighter bodywork and interior trim took a total 200lb (91kg) off the weight. Then the engine was equipped with a new twin-plug head and triple 45DCO Webers for which Aston Martin claimed 302bhp – it was actually nearer a still impressive 270bhp but the company had got involved in a horsepower race. Outwardly the car was distinguished by cowled headlights which helped to reduce drag.

Known internally as DP199 (Design Project) the still prototype car was raced at the 1959 International Trophy meeting at Silverstone where Stirling Moss won the first ever GT race at an average speed of 87mph (140km/h). The same car went to the Le Mans 24-hour race for the Swiss importer to run, but as it was entered as a prototype it had to use a 3-litre short-stroke version of the engine which was not a success; the bearings failed after an hour.

The DB4GT was finally launched at the Motor Show in October 1959 and 0-100-0mph (0-161-0km/h) in 20 seconds was claimed. Only a lightweight factory development car was tested by magazines and that reached 100mph (161km/h) in 14.2 seconds, but a standard one should have reached 100mph (161km/h) in 15 seconds and braked to zero in 5 seconds thanks to the new Girling brakes. Top speed was 150mph (241km/h) which, for 1959, made it a very fast car indeed. It was somewhat noisier than the standard car but could still be enjoyed on the open road.

Aston Martin followed this up a year later with the introduction of the DB4GT Zagato, commissioning the Milan-based coachbuilder to create one of his all-time great designs. It was another 100lb (45kg) lighter, thanks mainly to perspex windows and even thinner trim, and the

Below: With five inches (127mm) removed from a DB4 wheelbase, the GT became a two-seater. With 270bhp it was very fast. The DB5 would use the same cowled headlights.

SPECIFICATION	1962 DB4GT & ZAGATO
ENGINE	6-cylinder dohc, 3670cc
HORSEPOWER	270bhp (net) @ 6000rpm
TRANSMISSION	4-speed manual DB
CHASSIS	Steel sheet with tubular frame for aluminium body
SUSPENSION	Wishbone, live axle on coil springs
BRAKES	Servo-assisted disc
TOP SPEED	152mph (245km/h)
ACCELERATION	0-60mph (96km/h): 6.2sec 0-100mph (161km/h): 14.2sec

factory claimed another 10bhp for it due to a higher compression ratio. In *Autocar's* test, the mean maximum speed came to 152.3mph (245.1km/h) with 0-100mph (0-161km/h) in 14.1 seconds; it is not surprising that these figures are the same as those for the development DB4GT – it weighed the same and had a Zagato engine! In fact the Zagato version would have been measurably quicker than a standard DB4GT.

Above: Although the factory did not race the Zagato-bodied DB4GTs, they helped private entrants like John Ogier, who ran 1VEV and 2VEV. Below: The archetypal DB4GT Zagato was one of the Italian house's best ever.

Over the four-year period 75 DB4GTs were built, and there should have been 25 Zagato versions to make the necessary 100 to qualify for International GT racing. In fact only 19 were built at the time; at £5470 the Zagato was very expensive, £800 more than the DB4GT, partly because DB4GT chassis had to be sent out to Zagato; those being sold on the British market went back to the factory for final trimming while others went direct to the importers. The car illustrated on the following pages was built for an Italian and is unique in having vertical uncowled headlights. Either he wanted better night vision – angled plastic cowls are not good – or he wanted his DB4GT Zagato to look more like a Ferrari 250GT; he succeeded in both.

Production dates	1959-63

All pictures: In most respects this is like any of the 19 DB4GT Zagatos with the twin-plug heads and big Weber carburettors, and the fully instrumented binnacle. There were subtle differences from one car to the next but this example is the only one to have been built with exposed headlights like a DB4; from the side and rear it looks like a Ferrari 250GT but from the front it could only be an Aston Martin.

Aston Martin DB5

THE DB5 was the car that put Aston Martin on the world's aspirational map. James Bond used a heavily-gadgetted one in the film *Goldfinger*, and the model version was one of the most popular toy cars for many years. It became the car that every youngster always promised himself to show that he had arrived. The car that actually did most of the filming work was the prototype DB5, which had started life as a Series 5 DB4 Vantage.

Vantage engines became available for the Series 4 which began in September 1961. These had a claimed 266bhp from bigger SU carburettors, higher compression ratio and bigger valves – probably 250bhp. Most of the cars with this specification had the cowled front of the GT model and were known as DB4 Vantage. With the Series 5, which was also slightly longer for more interior space and had the GT's more comprehensive instrument panel, the majority of the cars were Vantage and five were Vantage GT, using the nominal 300bhp version.

By this time, the DB4 had visually defined the DB5 and the changeover was a gradual one in mid-1963; the car used for the launch was the former DB4 Vantage which would go on to feature in *Goldfinger*. But under the skin there were some more substantial changes which fully justified calling the DB5 a new model, rather than an extension of the DB4.

Below: The new DB5, with cowled lights and 4-litre power.

Above: Over 10 percent of the 1021 DB5s were built as convertibles during the two-year life of the James Bond car.

While Lagonda's arrival in the David Brown group had been significant in providing the DB2 engine and a fine stylist in Frank Feeley, the 3-litre Lagonda fell by the wayside as production became concentrated in Newport Pagnell with the start of DB4 manufacture. Once that was under way, David Brown insisted on reviving the Lagonda name with a stretched luxury DB4, also with Touring bodywork, and the Rapide arrived in 1961; its extra weight had required the DB4 engine to be increased in capacity to 4-litres by increasing the bore to 96mm (3.78in). It was this size that was used for the DB5 with triple SUs and a claimed 282bhp, about 40bhp more than the actual test-bed figures.

Significant too was the option of the ZF 5-speed gearbox. The David Brown 4-speed with a Laycock overdrive was standard, but a true 5-speed all-synchromesh was infinitely preferable and ZF would provide gearboxes for Aston Martin for many years to come. A 3-speed Borg Warner automatic transmission was also available. Other chassis changes included the adoption of the Girling disc brakes that had only been on the DB4GT, and 15-inch wheels to put more Avon rubber on the road.

Such features as Sundym glass and electric windows changed from DB4 options to standard fitments, while air conditioning became an option. The DB5 was definitely designed as a pure road car with no racing pretensions, although the outright performance was still impressive. A maximum speed of 143mph (230km/h) and 0-100mph (0-161km/h) in 17.5 seconds was almost as quick as the DB4GT with a lot more comfort; the option a year later of an extra 30bhp with triple Weber carburettors brought it even closer.

The ratio of convertibles was rising during the DB5's two years of production; 123 were built and Harold Radford made 12 shooting brakes (estate cars) out of the total 1021 DB5s.

Production dates	1963-65

SPECIFICATION	1964 DB5
ENGINE	6-cylinder dohc, 3995cc
HORSEPOWER	242bhp (net) @ 5500rpm
TRANSMISSION	5-speed manual ZF
CHASSIS	Steel sheet with tubular body frame
SUSPENSION	Wishbone, live axle on coil springs
BRAKES	Servo-assisted disc
TOP SPEED	143mph (230km/h)
ACCELERATION	0-60mph (96km/h): 7.4sec 0-100mph (161km/h): 17.5sec

41

Above: English coachbuilder Harold Radford built just 12 of these stylish shooting brakes, the first of the GTEs.

Aston Martin DB6

A FURTHER refinement of the DB4 design, the DB6 appeared in two phases following its launch at the 1965 Motor Show. In the period to July 1969, 1327 saloons were built; the Mk II then took over and 240 of these were built up to November 1970. Over the same period, 215 convertibles were built and the new bigger DBS arrived in September 1967. It was a period of considerable activity at Newport Pagnell.

Early in 1964 Aston Martin had finally moved out of Feltham, so the DB6 was the first car to be engineered at Newport Pagnell. For this model change, it involved structural rather than mechanical engineering. Market appeal would be increased if the new model could have more rear seat space, so another 4in (102mm) was inserted in the wheelbase just ahead of the rear wheel arches; this gave extra leg room while squatter rear seat

cushions and a raised roof line gave extra headroom; extra width came through shortening the upper trailing arm of the rear suspension to remove its mounting point from the seat squab area. The changes certainly made the back seat far more comfortable for adults.

The chassis platform was still being built in Huddersfield but the superstructure was no longer to Touring Superleggera licence; it was built up from sheet steel at Newport Pagnell. The DB6 was instantly recognisable from its predecessors by the fitment of a rear spoiler above a sharply cut-off Kamm tail; a product of earlier racing experience, this treatment usefully reduced rear-end aerodynamic lift. At the front, split bumpers flanked a large oil cooler intake. Mechanically the specification remained much the same as for the DB5; the triple SU version produced 240bhp (282bhp claimed) and

the Vantage 325bhp was actually 270bhp. The slight power increase and a lower drag shape combined to give the Vantage a maximum speed of almost 150mph (241km/h) and the ability to reach 100mph (161km/h) in 15 seconds.

Whichever model was chosen, the price was the same £4998, whether manual or automatic; power steering and air-conditioning were the only extras. The 1965 convertible was built on the short DB5 chassis and renamed Volante.

In July 1966 the Wilson government increased purchase tax and clamped down on hire purchase tax concessions. While this increased the DB6 price to £5084, the overall economic uncertainty cut back orders dramatically. In February 1967, David Brown was forced to slash £1000 off the price to try and reduce the stock pile that had built up. All this had considerable repercussions on Aston Martin's new model plans. The October 1966 Motor Shows saw a new Volante on the DB6 chassis complete with power hood, and a new Touring-designed high-speed two-seater called the DBS; this last was then dropped because it would have taken too long to engineer for production, so DBS was the name given to the new wider car whose launch would be brought forward to October 1967.

Come 1969 and the DB6 had a useful face-lift to enable it to share DBS components; the wider wheels and tyres required slight flares above the wheel arches and made a remarkable difference to the appearance. But by now the basic design was 12 years old and the world wanted bigger and faster machinery with greater comfort.

Production dates	1965-70

Opposite: Initially convertible DB6s were DB5s with a Volante name, but a year later Volantes adopted the longer DB6 wheelbase. This is a Mark II with the wider wheels.

Below: The lower car shows the first series DB6 with the Kamm tail, large oil cooler intake and longer wheelbase to give more rear seat space. The upper model is a Mark II with the wheel arches flared for the DBS wheels.

SPECIFICATION	1966 DB6 VANTAGE
ENGINE	6-cylinder dohc, 3995cc
HORSEPOWER	272bhp (net) @ 5750rpm
TRANSMISSION	5-speed manual ZF
CHASSIS	Steel sheet platform and frame for aluminium body
SUSPENSION	Wishbone, live axle on coil springs
BRAKES	Servo-assisted disc
TOP SPEED	148mph (238km/h)
ACCELERATION	0-60mph (96km/h): 6.3sec 0-100mph (161km/h): 15.5sec

Aston Martin DBS

SIR David Brown (knighted in 1968) had long wanted to take Aston Martin into the luxury league, but still remain a front runner in the performance stakes. A new engine was needed to achieve the task of pushing a bigger car through the air faster than the previous model. So Tadek Marek started work on a V8 of around 5-litres in 1963 while still based in Feltham. The brief was to retain as much of the proven components as possible, notably pistons, bearings and valve-gear in an all-aluminium twin-overhead-camshaft design.

Marek was head of a small engineering department of just 23 people who all had day-to-day duties in existing development projects, so progress was not fast. It was not until July 1965 that the engine first ran. By the end of the year the 4.8-litre V8 was producing a genuine 325bhp on Weber carburettors. Work continued during 1966 during which it was agreed that Lola would use Aston engines for some races in 1967 including the Le Mans 24-hour race. Le Mans proved to be a disaster for the Lola-Astons – they were both out early on –

but it was a triumph of development for the new V8. Valuable lessons were learnt; racing had improved the breed again.

Following a certain amount of redesign and durability running, the engine was finally brought into production in late 1969 in 5340cc form with Bosch fuel injection and a genuine 315bhp. It was the engine for which the DBS had been designed, but the market had forced that model into production two years earlier with the DB6 engine.

The government's punitive tax measures had come in July 1966. At the October Motor Show, the DB6 Volante was shown alongside the two-seater

Below: Just two DBSCs were built by Touring in Milan.

SPECIFICATION	1970 DBS V8
ENGINE	V8 dohc per bank, 5340cc
HORSEPOWER	315bhp @ 5000rpm
TRANSMISSION	5-speed manual ZF
CHASSIS	Steel sheet platform and frame for aluminium body
SUSPENSION	Wishbone, de Dion axle on coil springs
BRAKES	Servo-assisted disc
TOP SPEED	161mph (259km/h)
ACCELERATION	0-60mph (96km/h): 6.0sec 0-100mph (161km/h): 13.8sec

DBS; neither was to be the answer to Aston's spare capacity. Consideration had been given to a widened DB6 and to another Touring-bodied car but, at a meeting after the Show, it was decided to accept the four-seater DBS proposal of William Towns who had recently joined the company as an interior designer. And the new car had to be on the show stand the following year, a seemingly impossible target.

However, a certain amount of relevant development had been on-going so the engineers knew exactly where they were heading the moment the button was pressed. The DB6 chassis was widened by 4.5in (114mm), the front wheels were moved forward 1in (25mm) to enable the engine to fit behind the front cross-member, and a de Dion rear axle was installed using the DB6 linkages; there were a few other changes but the basic chassis layout was quickly established and the superstructure system was just the same as that for the DB6. The new chassis platform would still be produced in Huddersfield. The rest of the mechanical components came from the DB6, so it was the striking new body that was to take the longest to produce. Patterns came from the sculpted full-size clay model and these were used to produce the formers on which the aluminium panels were shaped.

Above: When the DBS was launched the V8 engine was not ready, so the DB6 engine was installed for two years.

The impossible target was met. The new DBS was on the show stand in October 1967 receiving wide acclaim for its spacious style, although it was another six months before owners could see how fast it went. Bigger and heavier than the DB6, it could only be slower, but 141.5mph (227.7km/h) and 0-100mph (0-161km/h) in 18 seconds were respectable figures. When the new engine was finally installed, a DBS V8 achieved 161mph (259km/h) and 0-100mph (0-161km/h) in 13.8 seconds, comfortably faster than its predecessor.

Production dates	1967-72

45

Aston Martin V8 Saloon & Volante

ONCE the DBS V8 had been launched, development continued with the aim of getting the V8 into the American market. But this was Sir David Brown's swansong. The tractor market had deteriorated and the parent company could no longer afford to support Aston Martin; it had never made a profit although it had been a useful marketing arm for the David Brown Group. Sir David sold Aston Martin Lagonda to Company Developments at the beginning of 1972 and William Willson took over as Chairman, bringing his own management team in. Inevitably all work

was now concentrated in Newport Pagnell and the company had to try and become self-supporting for the first time in its life.

It was to be the first of many changes of ownership during the 20-year life of the V8 saloon. The David Brown contribution was 405 DBS V8s and 830 DBS. Inevitably the new management had to remove the DB prefix and the two models became the AMV8 and the AM Vantage – a temporary loss of status for the Vantage which had always been the most powerful model. They also changed the front end to the single headlight style

that stayed with the car thereafter. After a further 250 V8s and 70 'sixes', the latter was dropped in July 1973 and a further revised V8 was brought out.

The major change in this was to drop the Bosch fuel injection in favour of four downdraught Weber carburettors which thus required a bigger bonnet bulge. It was looking difficult to get that early Bosch system through increasingly strict

Below: The V8 Volante came in response to American demand and was launched in 1978. This 1980 example demonstrates the timeless elegance in open form.

Left: The lined, power-operated hood gives a near-saloon feel to the interior.

Above: The 1978 demonstrator shows the first change to the DBS shape with a built-in spoiler and scoopless bonnet.

American emission laws. But, given the after effects of the Yom Kippur war, the company badly needed the US market. The V8 had been sold in the USA at the end of 1971 but could not pass the 1972 legislation. They had to wait again till 1974 before the new V8 with special Webers could pass the tests and the durability run that went with them; certification arrived in October 1974. The Motor Show that month had seen the launch of the four-door Aston Martin with a Lagonda badge; the one-off that Sir David Brown had had built was finally in production five years later.

This proved to be the swansong for Company Developments. Their property and secondary banking interests had taken a tumble, and, despite selling off some of the company assets, they put Aston Martin into the hands of the receiver at the end of 1974. Production stopped. By the middle of the year, new owners had arrived – American Peter Sprague and Canadian George Minden were later joined by Alan Curtis and Denis Flather. They relaunched the range for the 1975 Motor Show and were back in business from the beginning of 1976.

The V8 continued in its existing form with detail changes until 1978 when the body had a restyle with a revised bonnet – no scoop on top – and a tail section that included a small spoiler. Inspired by the American market, a drophead version returned as the new Volante in mid-1978 – a car of timeless elegance.

The V8 and Volante would continue in much the same 280-300bhp specification, until the return of fuel injection in 1986 which also allowed a flatter bonnet line. Despite the ever more demanding emission laws, the V8 had retained its 300bhp European output , but the arrival of fuel injection allowed the American market to enjoy the same performance.

In 1988 the new Virage was launched and the V8 saloon and its Volante sister went into retirement after all but 20 years in production and four fundamental changes of company ownership.

SPECIFICATION	1979 V8 VOLANTE (Auto)
ENGINE	V8 dohc per bank, 5340cc
HORSEPOWER	304bhp @ 5500rpm
TRANSMISSION	3-speed automatic, Borg Warner
CHASSIS	Steel sheet platform and frame for aluminium body
SUSPENSION	Wishbone, de Dion axle on coil springs
BRAKES	Servo-assisted disc
TOP SPEED	150mph (241km/h)
ACCELERATION	0-60mph (96km/h): 7.5sec 0-100mph (161km/h): 17.0sec

Production dates 1972-89

The Vantage engine, below, retained carburettors when the standard V8 engine was fitted with Weber fuel injection in January 1986. While the standard Volante and V8 were able to have flat bonnets, Vantage-engined Volantes had to have bonnet bulges, right, like this 1989 car. The model was offered with a more obvious body-kit but this Prince of Wales (POW) specification retained the normal Volante look with an open grille but had slightly flared arches. The interior, left, is typical of the high standards of Aston Martin trim with Connolly leather and contrasting piping.

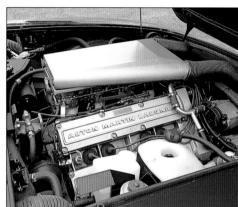

Aston Martin V8 Vantage

FOLLOWING the 1974 stop and restart, the new owners had ambitious plans to show the world that Aston Martin was back in production. The DBS shape had been around for eight years and they wanted to change it. William Towns was asked to design a modern looking replacement. At the beginning of 1976 he produced clay models of a two-door Aston and a stretched four-door version to carry the Lagonda name again. Willson's Lagonda had never got beyond assembly of the cars that were in production when the receiver came in – just seven cars in all.

The new owners chose to develop the Lagonda and to give it the latest in electronic instrumentation and switchgear to match its sleek razor-edged styling. Rushed into view for the 1976 Motor Show, it then took three years of development before it became a production feasibility. Celebrating the reprieve for the DBS shape, a new high performance addition to the range appeared in February 1977 – the Vantage was back.

The company had chosen one of the Aston Martin Owners Club race meetings to try the prototype. With new large downdraught Weber carburettors, new camshafts and bigger inlet valves, the faithful V8 turned out 370bhp. Aerodynamic drag was improved by blanking off the bonnet-top intake and filling in the grille thus concentrating cooling and intake air through a hole in the new under-bumper spoiler; at the rear, a tail-lip spoiler was grafted onto the back panel. Stiffer suspension and wider wheels improved its cornering power.

At this time the standard V8 was giving around 280bhp, so the 370bhp Vantage was significantly quicker. *Motor* estimated its maximum speed at 168mph (270km/h) and timed its 0-100mph (0-161km/h) at 13.0 seconds. This may not seem a lot faster than the original DBS V8 but the car had become somewhat heavier and the exhaust emissions were a lot lower. Besides, that first test car had 20bhp more than standard at 338bhp; Aston had become caught up in their own deceptions and had given up quoting horsepower when they launched the V8, so 20bhp more than an unknown figure could not be questioned.

Some of the Vantage lessons were passed on to the V8 which earned 305bhp. And the Vantage

Left: The Vantage was launched in 1977, a year before the major body changes. This 1977 factory press car shows the blanked-in air-scoop, filled-in grille and large air-dam.

Above: Rear of the 1977 Vantage shows the separate spoiler.

bodywork additions were integrated into the new bonnet and tail which went across the range in October 1978. The Vantage continued virtually unchanged for another seven years apart from ever wider tyres and appropriate wheel-arch flares. During this period Pace Petroleum with Victor Gauntlett and CH Industrials with Tim Hearley had taken over from the Sprague-Curtis consortium in 1981. In 1983, this transferred into Gauntlett and the Greek-owned Automotive Investments Inc until 1985, and then into Gauntlett plus Peter Livanos until the Ford take-over in 1987.

October 1986 saw the standard V8, and the Lagonda, receive Weber fuel injection but it was not worth engineering a separate system for the Vantage alone, so that stayed with carburettors. However, new large ones and further revised camshafts lifted the output to 400bhp with 432bhp available on the aftermarket with a big bore exhaust system – enough for 175mph (282km/h).

Production dates 1977-89

SPECIFICATION	1981 V8 VANTAGE
ENGINE	V8 dohc per bank, 5340cc
HORSEPOWER	375bhp @ 6000rpm
TRANSMISSION	5-speed manual ZF
CHASSIS	Steel sheet platform and frame for aluminium body
SUSPENSION	Wishbone, de Dion axle on coil springs
BRAKES	Servo-assisted disc
TOP SPEED	168mph (270km/h)
ACCELERATION	0-60mph (96km/h): 5.4sec 0-100mph (161km/h): 13.0sec

Aston Martin Vantage Volante

THE STANDARD Volante had done extremely well for the company since its June 1978 introduction. The American market took most of the first year's production and always chose more Volantes than V8 saloons. The Vantage was never put through emission testing; the nearest the American market could get was to have 'cosmetic Vantages' – Vantage lookalikes with unblanked grilles and standard engines.

When the range switched to the revised tail-spoiler bodywork in October 1978 bodywork, the Volante retained its original flat tail. Being a notchback, rather than a fastback coupé, its boot-lid was unique to itself. In the final phase of the V8 life, when it was common knowledge that a new car was on the way, something was needed to add a little more choice to the range.

The Volante's appeal was extended by offering Vantage power. The chassis had always proved plenty stiff enough, so it could handle the extra power, but it also needed to be able to take the stiffer suspension and wider wheels to become a true Vantage Volante, so the bodywork had to be modified – more than just by having the blanked-in grille and the carburettor bonnet.

While the wings could be flared like the saloon Vantage, it really also needed some sill skirts to stop stones being thrown up onto the paintwork by wheels which protruded beyond the bodywork – a Vantage problem; so glass-fibre skirts replaced the

Below: Vantage Volante was first shown in late 1986 with Vantage details plus exaggerated dam and arch flares.

Left: Part of the standard Vantage Volante package was the more pronounced rear spoiler on the boot deck.

chrome sill covers that had always been a feature of the cars. Then the front spoiler had to be modified to match the sills and finally the tail received a full-width lip spoiler. To those accustomed to many years of staid formality, the Vantage Volante was almost a caricature, but it looked the part it was trying to achieve.

Not everyone who wanted the extra power liked the body package that came with it. The Prince of Wales was one who preferred understatement. Such is the advantage of bespoke production that it is relatively easy to mix and match. The Prince of Wales' specification used Vantage power under a Vantage bonnet but the rest of the body was pure Volante.

While the V8 and Vantage ceased production in October 1989 in favour of the new Virage, the Volante continued until the end of that year. In the 11 years of its life, 849 were produced including the Vantage Volantes. Over the 20 years of DBS V8 to the final V8, 2308 cars were made, and a further 350

SPECIFICATION	1986 VANTAGE VOLANTE
ENGINE	V8 dohc per bank, 5340cc
HORSEPOWER	375bhp @ 6000rpm
TRANSMISSION	5-speed manual ZF
CHASSIS	Steel sheet platform and frame for aluminium body
SUSPENSION	Wishbone, de Dion axle on coil springs
BRAKES	Servo-assisted disc
TOP SPEED	162mph (261km/h)
ACCELERATION	0-60mph (96km/h): 5.8sec 0-100mph (161km/h): 13.8sec

Vantages were built over the twelve and a half years of its life.

These numbers are a drop in the ocean of the automotive world, but exclusivity is part and parcel of the Aston Martin appeal.

Production dates   1986-89

Aston Martin Vantage Zagato

NOBODY needed reminding of Zagato's previous connection with Aston Martin, least of all Victor Gauntlett when he found Aston Martin's Geneva Motor Show stand alongside that of coachbuilder Zagato in 1984. The DB4GT Zagatos were all-time greats in anyone's terms. Twenty-five years on, Aston's new owners were looking for a similar extension to the Vantage range. Founder Ugo Zagato had died, but the company was being run by his two sons, Dr. Elio and Ing. Gianni.

During the earlier Aston Zagato production and throughout the 'sixties and 'seventies, the Italian company was building niche models for various separate Italian manufacturers. By 1984, the major part of the Italian industry was controlled by Fiat, and Zagato needed to find work outside Italy. Shortly after that motor show meeting, the general specification for a new Zagato-bodied Aston Martin was agreed – given around 420bhp it had to be light enough to reach 60mph (96km/h) in under five seconds and aerodynamic enough to achieve

186mph (300km/h), with just two seats. Probable production would be 50 cars.

The Zagatos set to work and would probably have had a prototype ready for the 1985 Geneva show; unfortunately Aston Martin was then in the throes of separating from AII which resulted in the loss of six months before the decision was taken. So Geneva visitors only had a sketch to go on, but that, plus the Aston Martin and Zagato reputations, were enough to persuade 50 buyers to place deposits over the next six months.

Finally three prototypes were exhibited at the 1986 Geneva Show, and production of the 50 cars began shortly afterwards. Aston Martin sent a

Left: A 1987 Vantage Zagato shows off its Italian bodywork with the production power bulge.

54

SPECIFICATION	1986 VANTAGE ZAGATO
ENGINE	V8 dohc per bank, 5340cc
HORSEPOWER	432bhp @ 6200rpm (optional)
TRANSMISSION	5-speed manual ZF
CHASSIS	Steel sheet platform and frame for aluminium body
SUSPENSION	Wishbone, de Dion axle on coil springs
BRAKES	Servo-assisted disc
TOP SPEED	186mph (299km/h)
ACCELERATION	0-60mph (96km/h): 4.8sec 0-100mph (161km/h): 11.3sec

rolling chassis out to Italy, a working platform which had already been tested on the road. Zagato built a new superstructure, fitted the aluminium panels, trimmed the interior, painted the car and then sent it back to Newport Pagnell. While there were mixed feelings about the styling, there was no doubt about its appeal and it matched its performance claims.

The car that was offered to the press was the first prototype and the French magazine *Sport Auto* was the only one to record a true maximum speed. Using a piece of unopened motorway, they achieved 299km/h (185.8mph), only 1km/h short of the target. The 0-60mph (0-96km/h) figure came to 4.8 seconds – on target. The engine used was the 432bhp version that would later be offered as an option on the regular Vantage.

At the time that the specification was given to the Zagatos, it was the intention to fit fuel injection to the Vantage engine, but this was never completed. However, Zagato designed the bonnet around the lower profile of an injection system and

had to change this after the overall shape was finalized. The prototype's bulge was roughly shaped at Newport Pagnell; although Zagato designed a much less obtrusive bulge for the production cars, the press never forgot it and always drew attention to that bulge. How it should have looked could be told by looking at the subsequent Volante Zagato convertibles fitted with the less powerful injection engine under a nice flat bonnet.

Both Vantage and Volante were limited edition runs, 50 + 2 prototypes of the former, and 35 of the latter. Maybe they were not as beautiful as the 1960 car, but they were a far more effective marketing exercise.

Above: A lower drag body allowed a top speed of nearly 300km/h (186mph). Below: Zagato redesigned the interior and made special lightweight seats.

Production dates	1986-89

All pictures: Volante Zagatos were designed to use the fuel-injection V8 engine so they had nearly flat bonnets. They also had full side-windows. The front end, with moving headlamp covers, shows strong similarity to original Vantage Zagato sketches. Inevitably, some owners wanted Vantage engines so these cars have power-bulge bonnets, while others preferred the Vantage Zagato front end which could also be fitted by the factory. The power-operated roof is simple and effective and the rear quarterlight drops down into a well. Over 1986 to 1989, Zagato built 50 Vantage and 35 Volante versions.

57

Aston Martin Virage

WHILE the old V8 was still well liked, and always received good road test reports, it was too big and heavy for the current climate in the automobile industry. It was also expensive to build and much engineering time was expended in finding new components as various ones became unavailable; all low-volume manufacturers use components from other manufacturers, most of whom have a much shorter model life than the V8's 20 years.

It was finally time to build a replacement, just as each successive owner had promised over the past ten years. At the time, early 1986, Newport Pagnell was building the three V8 models on one basic chassis with original David Brown jigs and the Lagonda on a different chassis with its own jigs; the

Lagonda was much simpler to build than the developed DB4. The commonality which had been planned back in 1976 never happened. Now it would. The new Aston would use a shortened version of the Lagonda chassis and both cars would share all the components, some of which would be new.

So a two-door Lagonda was used for all the development work, just as William Towns had originally designed it. Using an established chassis meant that drawings could be produced very quickly for a selection of design engineers to create styling proposals. Five designers, including William Towns, were given four months in which to produce quarter-scale models for clinic evaluation on 28th August 1986. The final decision was announced

within the factory on 8th October, just two years before the planned launch; Royal College of Arts tutors Ken Greenley and John Heffernan won the contest with a design that was evolutionary but modern – work on the new body would start immediately.

The contract to develop the engine went to Callaway Engineering in Connecticut, USA, not far from the Aston Martin importership. It had to become a world engine capable of passing any emission laws with a single specification. The bottom half of the existing engine had proved unburstable in many racing applications so that was retained, but new heads were designed for it with four valves per cylinder and hydraulic tappets. It would eventually produce 330bhp using Weber electronic injection.

Below: 1989 Virage was the first new Aston for 18 years.

Above: In 1996, the Vantage-styled V8 became standard.

SPECIFICATION	1990 VIRAGE
ENGINE	V8 dohc per bank, 32-valve 5340cc
HORSEPOWER	335bhp @ 5300rpm
TRANSMISSION	5-speed manual ZF
CHASSIS	Steel sheet platform and frame for aluminium body
SUSPENSION	Wishbone, de Dion axle on coil springs
BRAKES	Servo-assisted disc
TOP SPEED	157mph (253km/h)
ACCELERATION	0-60mph (96km/h): 6.8sec 0-100mph (161km/h): 15.5sec

The chassis was evolved from the Lagonda but used revised wishbone front suspension and a new lighter de Dion system using aluminium castings for the beam and the triangulated arms which met at a big rubber-mounted ball-joint under the rear seat. This required the rear floor pan to be changed. The system was still located laterally by a Watt linkage.

Partway through the development Ford took over the majority shareholding, but were happy to leave the Virage in Aston's capable hands. The car met its launch date and was in production by the following autumn as the old cars were phased out. It achieved most of what it set out to do. It was quieter, more comfortable and more modern, but it was still big and not exactly light at 4320lb (1920kg).

Maximum speed came out at 158mph (254km/h) with 0-60mph (0-96km/h) in 6.5 seconds.

Virage production started well, and was reinforced by the Virage Volante, but by 1992 the recession had begun to bite and the big Aston was not everyone's ideal. The Volante and the new Vantage proved more attractive. The Virage coupé became the base for bespoke special editions, each with their own name, so much so that the name Virage quietly disappeared during 1994. As before the generic title became V8 for Volante, Vantage and in 1996, the Vantage-styled Coupé finally became the standard model.

Production dates 1989-94

Aston Martin Volante & Virage Derivatives

TRUE TO promised form the Virage Volante was launched at the Birmingham Motor Show in October 1990 and was hailed an instant success. The original Virage had been designed with the convertible in parallel; it had all the elegance that the previous V8 Volante had displayed in its own period. Unlike that, though, it was built as a two-seater leaving a luggage platform behind the front seats. With the same running gear as the Virage, performance was virtually the same.

Obviously it had a power-operated roof which sat rather too high on the early versions; however, this was improved by the time the 2+2 cabriolet was shown at Geneva in March 1992. That was a busy year on the Virage front. The same Geneva Show had seen a shooting brake conversion on the Virage frame; with the extra headroom afforded by the revised roof line, it was more of a full four-seater than the standard car. Customers could order them new or have existing Virages converted. This was the first shooting brake to be designed by the factory as the previous versions of DB5 and DB6 had been developed by outside specialists.

At the beginning of 1992, the Aston Service department announced high performance conversions of the Virage for those unwilling to wait for the Vantage. It was a comprehensive package. The engine capacity was increased to 6.3-litres with a bigger bore and a longer stroke, pistons and camshafts were changed, the engine management system was revised and the power rose to 465bhp taking the maximum speed to over 170mph (274km/h).

To handle this extra performance, suspension and anti-roll bars were uprated, race-developed brakes with an anti-lock system were specified and taller, wider wheels were fitted to take Goodyear 285/45 ZR 18 tyres – the wheel-arches had to be flared to accommodate them. All of which added around £50,000 to the price. October 1992 saw the real Vantage arrive, even faster and more outrageous than the 6.3 conversions, with production scheduled for 1993.

A useful change came in 1993 with the adoption of a 4-speed automatic transmission to complement the ZF 5-speed which could now be offered in 6-speed form. At the end of that year the Lagonda name came back on Virages that had been stretched 12in (305mm) by the service department to allow four doors, or even five as the estate could be stretched too. The previous Lagonda had undergone a face-lift in 1987 but had quietly disappeared in 1990 once the Virage was under way.

Continuing to emphasize the bespoke nature of Newport Pagnell production, a 10-off Limited Edition coupé came in October 1994 with a 10 percent power increase, anti-lock brakes and every

Left: The Virage Volante was launched in October 1990.

SPECIFICATION	1992 VIRAGE 6.3
ENGINE	V8 dohc per bank, 32-valve 6347cc
HORSEPOWER	465bhp @ 5800rpm
TRANSMISSION	5-speed manual ZF
CHASSIS	Steel sheet platform and frame for aluminium body
SUSPENSION	Wishbone, de Dion axle on coil springs
BRAKES	Discs all round with ABS
TOP SPEED	174mph (280km/h)
ACCELERATION	0-60mph (96km/h): 5.4sec 0-100mph (161km/h): 11.3sec

Left: The Volante roof limits rear seat space to +2 status.

Left: Aston Martin's Service Department revived the Lagonda name for four-door and Estate versions of Virage.

one was painted British racing green. The latest model arrived in March 1996, the Aston Martin V8 Coupé, with 350bhp and a new engine management system; bodily it was an understated Vantage with a different frontal aspect and wheels that were not quite as wide at 8.5 inches. The V8 Coupé is the Virage successor.

The recession gave the Virage a tough time but the Newport Pagnell factory responded with a succession of interesting variations that kept the flag of traditional craftsmanship flying and paved the way for the continued production of bespoke Astons.

Production dates   1991-date

Aston Martin Vantage

THE LATEST Aston Vantage is a far more brutal version of the original car than any Vantage has ever been since the name was coined back in 1951 to denote the DB2's more powerful engine. It was not until 1977 that Vantage became a separate model, recognizable at a glance from the blocked-in grille and deeper air-dam with wheel-arches flared to cover wider wheels.

The original Virage was not slow with a maximum speed around 157mph (253km/h), but it had a fair amount of weight to get under way, so the 0-60mph (0-96km/h) time was slow by Aston standards. And the Virage was designed for comfortable fast touring, so it lacked the handling tautness that the traditional Aston driver expects. The Vantage addressed these relative shortcomings

in full measure. The 6.3-litre option pack was a good half-way house.

The original Virage started with 335bhp, the 6.3 gave 465bhp, but the Vantage gives 550bhp with the standard size engine. For the last twenty years, the traditional way of increasing power has been to use turbo-charging, but this brings with it the problem of turbo-lag unless you use a number of little turbos. Aston Martin decided to revert to the 'thirties traditions of supercharging, where the units are directly driven by the engine and thus provide instant response. Using twin Eaton 'blowers' the

SPECIFICATION	1993 VANTAGE
ENGINE	V8 dohc, 32-valve supercharged 5340cc
POWER	550bhp @ 6500rpm
TRANSMISSION	6-speed manual ZF
CHASSIS	Steel sheet platform and frame for aluminium body
SUSPENSION	Wishbone, de Dion axle on coil springs
BRAKES	Discs all round with ABS
TOP SPEED	185mph (298km/h)
ACCELERATION	60mph (0-96km/h): 4.6sec 100mph (0-161km/h): 10.1sec

5.34-litre V8 now produces a massive 550bhp, but still has tremendous low-speed pull.

The traditional ZF 5-speed gearbox has been replaced by a 6-speed version; five gears are used to power the Vantage up to its maximum speed with sixth an overdrive, giving a very long-legged 42mph (68km/h) per 1000 rpm. *Autocar* testing saw 177mph (285km/h) in fifth gear around the Millbrook bowl and there was more to come; Aston Martin say the car has recorded 191mph (307km/h), so it is safe to say that the car can do at least 185mph (298km/h), which is the point at which the engine develops its maximum power in 5th gear. In acceleration, the new Vantage is very quick despite weighing nearly two tons; 0-60mph (0-96km/h) in 4.6 seconds and 0-100mph (0-161km/h) in 10.1 seconds make it comfortably the quickest Aston yet. Despite that, it remains a very tractable car to drive around town.

Left and right: New Vantage displays a revised air dam and muscular flanks. The front features ellipsoidal lamps.

Inevitably the chassis has been modified to cope with this extra performance; the changes follow the work done on the 6.3 option, many of which have been carried through to the others in the range. The suspension has been considerably stiffened to keep roll angles down which makes the ride somewhat bouncy, but the handling is all that you expect and want from a powerful rear-wheel-drive sports car; the front responds well to the steering and the back answers to the throttle.

The body style follows the 6.3 fairly closely with its spoiler and the flared arches but the 'face' is different with a battery of three small lights flanking a different grille. Since the arrival of the DB4 in 1958, Aston Martin have always fielded a contender near the front of the supercar league; despite the fact that most of the recent supercars have been mid-engined, the Aston Martin Vantage is still in the same league.

Production dates	1992-date

Above: The Vantage engine gives 550bhp against standard 335bhp, thanks to twin belt-driven Eaton superchargers, which give more controllable power than would turbos.

Aston Martin DB7

THE SIX-cylinder DB6 Mk II ceased production in November 1970. Twenty-four years on, DB7 has extended the range; Sir David was delighted to be brought back into the Aston fold as patron and readily allowed his initials to be used for the new small car.

Throughout the 'eighties, Victor Gauntlett and his various partners had recognized that an entry-level Aston 2+2 was needed to take the company's sales into the higher volume world of the Porsche 928 and Mercedes SL. Despite a steady increase in Aston fortunes, the company was not in a position to afford the design and production of a new car, even though it would still have to borrow a number of parts from existing higher-volume manufacturers. When Ford took a majority shareholding in 1987 this began to look possible. When Ford absorbed Jaguar in 1989, the possibility moved to a probability.

Jaguar had intended to replace the XJS with the new XJ41 once the XJ40 – the 1986 XJ6 – was in production. A number of XJ41 prototypes had been built before it was decided that the production cost would be too high for Jaguar volumes; as a low-cost alternative, Jaguar put the XJ41 body onto the existing XJS platform. Ford axed this one too, but it was to provide an excellent basis for a small Aston Martin which could be priced at a more realistic level with lower sales volumes. Work started on the Aston version – Project NPX – at the end of 1991. The body style was to be redefined by Ian Callum, working for the independent TWR Group who would build the prototypes and set up the production line in a new factory at Bloxham.

With the future of the company now assured, and the DB7 under way, Victor Gauntlett handed over the chairmanship to Ford's Walter Hayes in late

Right: The DB7 was styled to look every inch a traditional Aston by TWR's Ian Callum.

1991. He had picked the company up when it was suffering in 1981 and had guided it through recovery to modest profit; he had launched the first new Aston in 20 years and had brought in Ford in 1987 to set up the future. Peter Livanos stayed on as a minority shareholder for another two years. Their contribution to the Aston Martin legend had been considerable.

The DB7's design and development time was considerably shortened by using established Jaguar componentry, particularly with the engine. The six-cylinder, twin-overhead-cam, four-valve Jaguar AJ-6 engine formed a logical progression from the DB2-6 range, provided it could be 'Astonized'. This was achieved by taking an unique 3.2-litre version of the AJ-6 engine and adding a supercharger to give 335bhp, close enough to the Mercedes 500SL V8 at 320bhp and the Porsche 928 S4 at 350bhp, and enough to power the DB7 to over 160mph (257km/h).

Forgetting the mixed heritage, and you cannot actually see any Jaguar components, the new Aston

SPECIFICATION	1994 DB7
ENGINE	6-cylinder, 24-valve supercharged 3239cc
POWER	335bhp @ 5600rpm
TRANSMISSION	5-speed manual Getrag
CHASSIS	Pressed steel
SUSPENSION	All-independent with wishbones
BRAKES	Discs all round with ABS
TOP SPEED	161mph (259km/h)
ACCELERATION	0-60mph (96km/h): 5.8sec 0-100mph (161km/h): 14.4sec

provides exactly what was required for a little sister to the V8 range. It has the looks, the comfort and the performance that one would expect from an Aston. As with the previous range, the Volante was planned alongside the coupé. Reflecting its biggest potential market place, this was revealed simultaneously at the Detroit and Los Angeles Shows in January 1996; the launch also signified the availability of the coupé in America.

By that time some 650 DB7 coupés had been built in the first full year of production; with 100 V8 variants, 1995 was a record year for the company. The previous best had been in 1964 when 591 DB5 models were built at Newport Pagnell. The decision to embark upon the small Aston project needed little justification, but the numbers now prove that it was essential for Aston Martin's survival.

Production dates   1994-date

Above: The fastback style leaves little headroom in the rear seat but the DB7 can be used as a 2+2 for children.

Below: The interior is hand-crafted as for all Aston Martins.

All pictures: The DB7 had been launched in 1994. The Volante followed in January 1996, launched simultaneously in Detroit and Los Angeles; the DB7 coupé also became available in the USA at the same time, denoting the importance of that market to Aston Martin. As the Volante arrived, Aston Martin production reached the highest ever in its 80-year history – 650 coupés and 100 traditional V8s overtook the 1964 figure of 591 DB5.

N476 GNM

Aston Martin DB3 & DB3S

Below: DB3S/9 was one of the factory team cars for 1956 when it finished second at Le Mans in the hands of Stirling Moss and Peter Collins. Here it is at Goodwood in 1994.

LIKE MOST of the company owners before him, David Brown believed in the value of competition as a means of promoting Aston Martin and its products. The DB1 and DB2 competed in their own classes; they were never contenders for outright victory. To change all that, Eberan von Eberhorst was brought in to design a purpose-built vehicle using DB2 components where appropriate. John Wyer would continue to run the race-team.

Von Eberhorst had been involved in the pre-war Auto-Union Grand Prix team, a fact which was reflected in the design of the new car. A twin-tube ladder frame had trailing-arm front suspension with a de Dion axle carried by trailing arms and a Panhard rod; transverse torsion bars were used at both ends. The engine was the familiar 2.6-litre DB2 unit with 133bhp on Weber carburettors when the DB3 belatedly took to the track at the 1951 Tourist Trophy, where it retired.

For 1952, they had a full season. The first outing at Silverstone in May saw three cars finishing 2-3-4 behind Stirling Moss' C-Type Jaguar, winning the 3-litre class and getting the Team Prize. At the end of the season, a lone survivor won the Goodwood 9-hour race, but there was not much success in between.

Over the winter of 1952/3 the team accepted that the car had to be designed down to a much lighter weight and that it needed more power. Work started on the DB3S in January using a similar concept but all the metal gauges were lighter, the

chassis was set lower and had a 6in (152mm) shorter wheelbase; the front suspension remained the same but the de Dion was located by a central slide rather than the Panhard rod. The new car was 165lb (75kg) lighter than the DB3. More power came from the 3-litre DB2 engine tuned to 160bhp against the 2.6-litre 140bhp; by the time the DB3S arrived for Le Mans 1953, the output was up to 180bhp. The DB3S was clothed in a magnificent Frank Feeley body.

With a little more power the DB3 did quite well for its last two races with a second in the Sebring 12 hours and a 3-4 in the Silverstone sports car race. After a poor debut at Le Mans, the DB3S swept the board for the remainder of 1953 winning the Isle of Man British Empire Trophy, Silverstone (1, 2, 3), Goodwood 9-hours (1, 2) and the TT (1 ,2).

Throughout 1953 the engineering team had been working on a Lagonda with a 4.5-litre V12 to rival the Ferraris. It was to prove a disaster and badly affected development of the DB3S, which thus had a bad 1954 while the team tried to run Lagondas and Astons. A DB3S 1, 2, 3 at Silverstone stood out among a string of retirements at other events. This did not stop the factory from offering production versions of the DB3S from October 1954; with 180bhp, these were not quite as powerful as the works cars, but many privateers enjoyed their racing with them. They were also one of the most beautiful sports cars of all time.

With a more concentrated effort, the DB3S fared much better in 1955. Twin plug heads had increased the power to 225bhp the previous season, and the engine was now further developed to 240bhp. Disc brakes were fitted for the first time.

British races saw the Astons always ahead of the Jaguars including a third win in the Goodwood 9-hours. Second place at Le Mans was a good International result and was repeated in 1956, a season that generally was not quite as good as the previous year as work was proceeding on the purpose-designed DBR1 for the next season.

Of 10 DB3, the works ran five, and there were 10 works DB3S out of a total 30 built.

Production dates	1951-56

SPECIFICATION	1952 DB3	1956 DB3S
ENGINE	6-cylinder dohc, 2580cc	6-cylinder dohc, 2922cc
HORSEPOWER	138bhp @ 5500rpm	230bhp @ 6000rpm
TRANSMISSION	4-speed DB	4-speed DB
CHASSIS	Twin-tube ladder, smaller tubes support aluminium body	
SUSPENSION	Trailing arms, de Dion axle, torsion bar springing	
BRAKES	Hydraulic drum	4-wheel disc
TOP SPEED	132mph (212km/h)	146mph (235km/h)
BEST RACE RESULTS	1st Goodwood 9-hour 1952	1st Goodwood 9-hour 1953/5 2nd Le Mans 24-hour 1955/6

Above: Forerunner of the DB3S, the DB3 was rarely a contender for victory; the older, heavier car's developed DB2 engine was less powerful than would be the case for the DB3S. DB3/5, here, won the 1952 Goodwood nine-hour race with Collins/Griffith.

69

Aston Martin DBR1, DBR2 & DBR4

WHILE the DB3 and DB3S had been built to race in their class in production sports car categories, their engine size was a limiting factor when it came to bidding for outright victory on the International scene; Jaguar and Ferrari had bigger engines. Despite that they did pretty well on the home front and had come close at Le Mans in 1955.

The DBR1 was designed without having to use production components, although the suspension followed the DB3 theme. A lightweight space-frame chassis carried trailing-arm front suspension and a de Dion axle, both ends using torsion bar springing. New bodywork was even sleeker than that of the DB3S. The engine used an aluminium, dry-sump, seven-bearing block mated to

the DB3S twin-plug cylinder head, which gave almost as much power in its initial 2.5-litre form as did the DB3S 3-litre. Le Mans 1956 forced prototypes to use 2.5-litre engines and the sole DBR1 was 7th before retiring after 20 hours.

For 1957, prototype capacities were again unrestricted so the DBR1 went up to its original 3-litre design, and had a fairly good year with Tony Brooks winning two races at Spa and the Nurburgring 1000km race. Le Mans saw the start of gearbox problems which were to dog the DBR1 and the two cars failed to finish. Nor did the new DBR2, although it made a promising start. This was the racing debut of the DB4 engine, more than a year ahead of its announcement; it was installed in the

aborted Lagonda V12 second-generation chassis from which the DBR1 was derived in smaller form. With more power from its bigger engine it was generally faster than the DBR1 over short races, but for 1958 it could only be used in national events as the International sports cars were limited to 3-litres.

With the new 3-litre limit the DBR1 should have won everything in 1958 as more power had been added with a wide-angle head, but motor racing never goes according to plan. A repeat victory at the Nurburgring (Moss) and a 1, 2, 3 at the Goodwood TT made up for failures at Sebring, the Targa Florio and Le Mans where an engine failure, a gearbox failure and a crash intervened – the Whiteheads were second, however, in an ex-works DB3S. The DBR2s clocked two home wins but lost out to a Lister-Jaguar at Spa.

That year should have seen Aston's Grand Prix car, the DBR4, competing while front-engined cars still had a chance. It had a space-frame but used wishbone front suspension and a de Dion at the rear, while the engine was a developed version of the original DBR1 2.5-litre unit. But the team concentrated on the sports cars. For 1959 it was to be the GP car's turn, with the sports cars taking a back seat apart from a full-scale attack on Le Mans.

However Moss borrowed a single car for the Nurburgring 1000km

Left: Aston Martin's DBR4 arrived in Grand Prix racing too late. By 1959, the winners were using mid-engined cars.

SPECIFICATION	1959 DBR1	1958 DBR2
ENGINE	6-cylinder dohc, 2992cc	6-cylinder dohc, 3910cc
HORSEPOWER	250bhp @ 6000rpm	300bhp @ 5800rpm
TRANSMISSION	5-speed DB	5-speed DB
CHASSIS	Twin-tube ladder, smaller tubes support aluminium body	
SUSPENSION	Trailing arms, de Dion axle, torsion bar springing	
BRAKES	4-wheel disc	4-wheel disc
TOP SPEED	158mph (254km/h)	164mph (264km/h)
BEST RACE RESULTS	1st N'ring 1000km (1957/8/9) 1st Tourist Trophy (1958/9) 1st Le Mans 24-hours (1959)	2nd Spa (1958)

Below: The DBR1 was the most successful of all racing Astons, giving David Brown the 1959 World Sports Car Championship including victory at Le Mans. Here, Simon Draper drives his 1958 DBR1 at the Goodwood Festival of Speed in 1994.

and won again. Then Le Mans came with a three-car team. Moss, with a more powerful engine, acted as hare to the Ferraris which duly expired, as did Moss' engine, but it left the way open for his team-mates to record a 1, 2 with Salvadori/Shelby taking the flag in Aston's finest victory. That left the team with a chance of winning the overall Sports Car Championship if they could win the Goodwood Tourist Trophy. Despite a pit-stop fire putting the lead car out, Moss took over the Shelby/Fairman car and won the race and the World Sports Car Championship with it. Astons then retired from sports car racing while on top.

Meanwhile the DBR4 had shown promise at the non-championship Silverstone race with a second, but Salvadori's two 6th places were the best for the rest of the year. The new DBR5 was never fast enough for 1960 and only ran in three races before being withdrawn. It was a sad end to a momentous decade of racing for Aston Martin.

Production dates   1956-60

All pictures: The DBR2 was an enlarged DBR1 built up around the chassis designed for the Lagonda V-12 sports-racing cars. Most of the suspension came from the DBR1 but the engine was the prototype DB4 being raced a year *before production. The factory raced them in 1957 and 1958, but the arrival of the 3-litre sports car formula in 1958 saw development switch to the DBR1, although the DBR2 did well in national events. The two DBR2s went* *to America with 4.2-litre versions of the DB4 engine and raced with considerable success. The pictures on these pages show the stunning 1957 Aston Martin DBR2, chassis number 1.*

The Project Cars

ALTHOUGH Aston Martin had withdrawn from sports car racing at the end of 1959, GT racing was to be another matter. The prototype DB4GT had won on its first outing in May 1959 and was launched in October 1959. Privateers would be encouraged to race both them and the Zagato versions that followed a year later. John Ogier's Essex Racing Team tried hard with both but usually had to give best to the Ferrari 250GTs. Under pressure from the dealers, Aston Martin agreed to build a special car for Le Mans 1962 – Project 212.

The regulations for Le Mans that year included a 4-litre prototype GT category, alongside the production GT cars for which the world championship was then being run. Project 212 used a lightened DB4GT platform with a de Dion axle on torsion bars, but the body was an all-new slippery coupé shape which could easily have been a four-seater – it really looked like a prototype for a production car. Its engine was the DB4GT unit taken out to the full 4-litres and fitted with bigger Weber carburettors to produce 327bhp.

Entered for Graham Hill and Richie Ginther it was very fast; it led the field at the end of the first lap and was second behind the winning prototype Ferrari 330P at the end of the first hour, but electrical problems dropped it down the field and an oil line broke after five hours. It was encouraging enough for the engineers to use the car as a test-bed for the following season. The car was very fast but aerodynamically unstable so the body was reshaped with a cut-off Kamm tail carrying a little spoiler above it.

This development was carried over to three new cars which had longer, lower and wider bodies terminating in the Kamm tail. Two Project 214 cars were run as special-bodied DB4GTs, despite the fact that the chassis platform was somewhat different and the engine was moved back; for these an extra 1mm (0.04in) bore gave a 3750cc capacity and 317bhp. The sole Project 215 used a similar chassis, but even lighter, and was scheduled to run as a GT prototype with the 4-litre engine, independent wishbone rear suspension and a 5-speed transaxle from the DBR1.

Le Mans 1963 was the first outing for all of them. In practice Innes Ireland in one of the Project 214s was the first person to clock 300km/h (186mph) on the long Mulsanne straight. But in the race both the 214s were put out with broken pistons – forged pistons were not ready so cast ones were used – and 215 was out before them with transmission problems. One of the 214s had reached 3rd position after 10 hours, at which point only prototypes were ahead of them, so the cars definitely had promise.

Left: One of the two Project 214 cars seen at Goodwood.

Project 215 ran once more at Rheims but it was retired after just four laps when Schlesser had gear selection problems, missed a change and dropped a valve. The two 214s ran on four more occasions as works cars. Ireland took 6th and 2nd GT (behind Sears' Ferrari GTO) at the Guards Trophy meeting and then 7th at the Tourist Trophy where the scrutineers had insisted on the cars using narrow DB4GT wheels with adverse effect on the handling. The Project cars' finest hour was in the 3-hour GT race preceding the Italian Grand Prix at Monza in September that year; Roy Salvadori beat

Below: Project 212 was built as a GT prototype in 1962.   *Above: Project 215's profile demonstrates aerodynamics.*

Mike Parkes' Ferrari 250GTO on its home ground after an epic battle; Lucien Bianchi brought the second car into third place. The final race at Montlhéry was a tribute to the Paris dealer; two French drivers finished in a 1, 2 to round off the Project cars' programme. It was the last year that race cars were prepared on Aston soil.

Production dates	1962-63

SPECIFICATION	1963 PROJECT 214
ENGINE	6-cylinder dohc, 3750cc
HORSEPOWER	310bhp @ 6000rpm
TRANSMISSION	4-speed manual DB
CHASSIS	Steel platform with tubular frame for aluminium body
SUSPENSION	Wishbone, live axle on coil springs
BRAKES	4-wheel disc
TOP SPEED	186mph (300km/h)
BEST RACE RESULT	1st Monza 3-hours (1963)

75

Aston Martin Bulldog

BULLDOG was a long time a-coming. When William Towns had finished work on the clay models for the razor-edged Lagonda in mid-1976, he was asked to lay down a mid-engined Super Aston – the term 'supercar' had yet to be coined. Towns had to finish his work by the end of that year and Mike Loasby, then in charge of the Engineering Department, had to work on the interior and the chassis. It was planned to launch Bulldog – the name chosen to convey British and best – as a driveable concept car for October 1978.

Loasby's design emerged as a multi-tube space-frame carrying de Dion axles front and rear, although the front one gave way to wishbones. The engine would be a highly developed V8. Inside, the latest in LCD technology was used for the instruments with digital readouts, but the interior was trimmed in traditional leather. Towns' bodywork was futuristic with large glass areas, big gull-wing doors and luggage space either side of the engine.

At that time, the Lagonda required a lot of work to inch it towards production, so Bulldog took a back seat despite the work being carried out off-site under Loasby's direct control. By the hoped-for launch date it was still only partly completed, and then Loasby left to join Delorean, so work stopped again. It was picked up again the following year by Keith Martin, who cordoned off an area within the engineering department and turned the car into working reality. By its final launch in April 1980 the V8 had grown twin turbochargers, as a Lagonda prototype would later do in an attempt to provide power without harmful emissions. Given its head, the engine could develop over 700bhp and 191mph (307km/h) was clocked at the motor industry test track at Nuneaton. Bulldog was certainly a working prototype which saw many miles on the test tracks and in promotions.

The Sprague/Minden/Curtis axis were keen to promote the engineering ability of Aston Martin to a wider customer base than just Newport Pagnell. As CHI and Pace joined the shareholding equation in mid-1980, Aston Martin Tickford was launched with Bulldog as the flagship to show what the small engineering team was capable of doing for a customer. The Tickford Metro and Tickford Capri were among the company's early projects.

Below: Bulldog was conceived in 1976 to demonstrate Aston Martin's engineering ability. With a turbocharged, mid-mounted V8 it was futuristic in style as well as instrumentation.

Shortly after AII took over the Pace Petroleum investment, Tickford was absorbed by the other shareholder, CHI, and Aston Martin was left without an internal engineering department, apart from a few personnel who stayed on as the core for subsequent expansion. While initially there were hopes that Bulldog would go into limited production, this never got near to being a reality and only the one car was ever built. It is still going strong.

Production dates	Only one built – 1978-80

The sole Bulldog was finally completed in 1980 and proved dramatically fast. These views emphasize the double wedge lines penned by William Towns who designed the DBS.

SPECIFICATION	1980 BULLDOG
ENGINE	V8 dohc per bank, turbocharged 5340cc
HORSEPOWER	580bhp @ 6200rpm
TRANSMISSION	5-speed manual ZF
CHASSIS	Tubular longerons, smaller tubes support aluminium body
SUSPENSION	Wishbone, de Dion axle on coil springs
BRAKES	4-wheel disc
TOP SPEED	195mph (314km/h)
ACCELERATION	0-60mph (96km/h): 5.1sec 0-100mph (161km/h): 10.1sec

Aston Martin Nimrod & AMR-1

MOTOR racing had done much for the Aston Martin name in the 'fifties, and the Project cars had been impressive enough. The 1967 Lola-Aston had been a useful exercise in development if not promotion; by the start of the 'seventies the V8 was strong enough to be a very raceworthy unit, but the company did not want to get involved in running a works team, although they were happy to assist privateers. One such was Aston dealer Robin Hamilton, who developed a V8 coupé to extremes and ran at Le Mans in 1977 with a factory-prepared engine developing 480bhp; some of this work rubbed off on the Vantage. The car finished the 24 hours in 17th place A return two years later with the car turbocharged and lowered saw weight and higher speeds prove too much for the brakes.

However, Hamilton was moving towards making a genuine mid-engined sports racer to compete in the new Group C World Championship. With Pace Petroleum involvement and Aston Martin blessing, the Nimrod-Aston arrived in time for the 1982 season using a chassis developed by Lola and V8 engines from Aston Martin Tickford. As it was planned to race in the USA and to sell to privateers, five cars were laid down. Once the racing started, Hamilton's 'works' car was always eclipsed by Lord Downe's private Nimrod run by Richard Williams; the Hamilton car usually started faster but the Downe car always finished in that first year, including a 7th at Le Mans, and finally took third in the world championship. Over the winter, however, Nimrod was running out of funds.

While the Hamilton team tried to keep going by racing in America for 1983, the Downe team attracted Bovis sponsorship, allowing Ray Mallock to develop a more effective and lighter body. Good results eluded them that year but the EMKA-Aston, another privateer project, claimed 17th at Le Mans. Two Nimrods ran under Bovis colours for 1984 but neither finished at the first race at Silverstone and both were sadly eliminated in the same accident at Le Mans when running well. That was the last time the Nimrods raced.

Mallock and Williams continued racing together under the Ecurie Ecosse banner in Group C2 over the next three years with considerable success, but they maintained a rolling plan for an Aston come-back should the finance ever become available. That this happened was entirely due to the enthusiasm and generosity of Peter Livanos, co-owner of Astons at the time with an equally enthusiastic Victor Gauntlett. Livanos, via Aston Martin, would fund the initial stages of design and development and Aston Martin would decide if the car was competitive enough to enter the world championship as an Aston. During 1987, Ecosse C2 designer Max Boxstrom drew up the whole AMR-1 which Mallock subsequently developed. It used such state-of-the-art features as carbon-fibre monocoque and bodywork. An unique gearbox was

Left: The Nimrod Aston Martin is seen in its final form as developed by Ray Mallock with Bovis sponsorship.

SPECIFICATION	1983 NIMROD	1989 AMR-1
ENGINE	V8 dohc per bank, 5340cc	V8 dohc 32-valve, 5998cc
HORSEPOWER	570bhp @ 7000rpm	670bhp @ 7000rpm
TRANSMISSION	5-speed Hewland	5-speed AMR
CHASSIS	Aluminium monocoque	Carbon-fibre monocoque
SUSPENSION	Wishbone independent	Wishbone independent
BRAKES	4-wheel disc	4-wheel carbon disc
TOP SPEED	213mph (343km/h)	217mph (349km/h)
BEST GP.C RESULTS	4th Silverstone 1000km (1982) 4th Le Mans 24-hour (1982)	4th B. Hatch 480km (1989) 6th Donington 480km (1989)

mated to a 6-litre version of the Aston V8 using the four-valve heads which were announced with the Virage in October 1988, almost coincidental with completion of the first AMR-1.

Aston Martin, through Proteus Technology, duly entered the 1989 World Championship using a single car for half the races. Dijon saw 17th and Le Mans 11th, but a lot of development in between produced a 4th at Brands Hatch. Donington with 6th and 7th was the best of the two-car entries. By the end of the season the team were 6th overall and highly respected. Outside forces then intervened. Le Mans 1990 looked very doubtful over that winter, and success at Le Mans meant more for Aston Martin than the championship; then Ford, who had promised Aston Martin the 3.5-litre Cosworth engine for the new formula for 1991, bought Jaguar and changed their minds. With possibly no Le Mans, and no 1991 engine, the Aston Martin race-team had little future and was disbanded in February 1990 before the new AMR-2 had taken shape. It was a sad end.

Below: The 'works' Nimrod team ran in 1982. Here is the Lees/Evans/Needell car at Le Mans before its accident.

Above: The factory-backed AMR1 team only ran in 1989 but achieved good results. AMR1/1 is here at Le Mans.

Production dates   1982-89

Index